THE COMPLETE
IRISH PUB
COOKBOOK

THE COMPLETE
IRISH PUB
COOKBOOK

The best of traditional and contemporary Irish cooking

First published 2012 by Parragon Books, Ltd.

Copyright © 2018 Cottage Door Press, LLC
5005 Newport Drive
Rolling Meadows, Illinois 60008

LOVE FOOD is an imprint of Cottage Door Press, LLC.

LOVE FOOD and the accompanying heart device are trademarks of
Cottage Door Press, LLC.

ISBN: 978-1-68052-412-3

New recipes by Christine McFadden
Home economy by Lincoln Jefferson
New photography by Mike Cooper
Cover design by Geoff Borin

Notes for the Reader
This book uses standard kitchen measuring spoons and cups. All spoon and
cup measurements are level unless otherwise indicated. Unless otherwise
stated, milk is assumed to be whole, eggs are large, individual fruits and
vegetables are medium, pepper is freshly ground black pepper, and salt is
table salt. A pinch of salt is calculated as 1/16 of a teaspoon. Unless
otherwise stated, all root vegetables should be peeled prior to using.

The times given are an approximate guide only. Preparation times differ
according to the techniques used by different people, and the cooking
times may also vary from those given.

Picture acknowledgments
The publisher would like to thank Getty Images for permission to
reproduce copyright materials:
7 Brian Lawrence; 9 The Edge Digital Photography; 16 Neale Clarke; 27,
122 David Cordner; 28 Comstock; 29 William Huber; 32 Frank Krahmer; 36
Ed Freeman; 51 Firecrest Picture; 60 Dennis Flaherty; 64, 93, 107, Design
Pics/The Irish Image Collection; 65 Tetra Images; 78 Douglas Pearson; 79
Chris Hill; 102, 119, 124, 146, 167, 168 IIC/Axiom; 106 Andy Goss; 113
Greg Gawlowski; 123 Diego Uchitel; 135 Stockbyte; 137 Altrendo travel;
154 Gerard Loucel; 155 Gill C. Kenny; 173 John Coveney

Contents

Introduction

Irish hospitality is world-renowned and can be sampled at its best in the traditional pub. Found in tiny villages, market towns, and bustling cities, each pub is unique and reflects the community it serves. Pubs come in all shapes and sizes—from tiny thatched buildings nestled in the hills, to splendid Victorian buildings with wood paneling, and stained glass. Whatever its size or location, the pub is the place where everyone, locals and visitors alike, can meet, relax, share a joke or two, and sample the local beverages.

As well as being the hub of their communities, pubs in Ireland increasingly reflect the best of Irish cooking. This has been transformed in recent years as skillful local cooks, inspired by the wealth of wonderful local produce, have created delicious new dishes and given new twists to favorite classics. This collection contains the best of both traditional and contemporary recipes and will enable you to cook up a truly Irish feast at home.

The four chapters in this book follow the course of a typical meal in an Irish pub. You can start by selecting from the delicious range of Appetizers & Snacks. Maybe a light salad featuring some of Ireland's famous seafood, or a hearty winter soup? For an Entrée, there's a choice of homely, traditional dishes like Irish Stew or something more impressive for a celebration, such as the whole baked sea trout. To accompany these is a great selection of Vegetables & Sides. The final chapter, Desserts & Drinks, includes sweet treats, plus the best of Irish baking, and some delicious drinks—the perfect way to round off any meal.

Chapter 1
APPETIZERS & SNACKS

Irish Buttermilk Pancakes

Nothing goes to waste in the Irish kitchen, including buttermilk—the thin liquid left over after churning butter. It has a pleasing, tangy flavor and is a main ingredient in Irish baking. Similar to drop biscuits in thickness, buttermilk pancakes have a slightly crisp, golden crust and a fluffy center.

Makes 12

1$\frac{1}{3}$ cups all-purpose flour
$\frac{3}{4}$ tablespoon sugar
$\frac{1}{2}$ teaspoon salt
1 teaspoon baking soda
1 egg, lightly beaten
1$\frac{1}{2}$ cups buttermilk
3 tablespoons vegetable oil, plus extra
   for brushing

To serve
$\frac{2}{3}$ cup heavy cream, whipped
1 cup blueberries

- Sift the flour, sugar, salt, and baking soda into a mixing bowl.

- Mix the egg with the buttermilk and vegetable oil in a large pitcher. Add to the dry ingredients, beating to a smooth, creamy batter. Let stand for at least 30 minutes or up to 2 hours.

- Heat a nonstick skillet or flat griddle pan over medium heat and brush with vegetable oil. Pour in enough batter to make 4-inch circles (about $\frac{1}{4}$ cup per pancake). Cook for 1$\frac{1}{2}$–2 minutes per side, or until small bubbles appear on the surface. Remove to a dish and keep warm while you cook the rest.

- Serve with softly whipped cream and blueberries.

Leek & Potato Soup

Leeks and potatoes are staples in Irish cuisine. For cooking, small, tender leeks are better than huge ones. This soup can be coarsely blended to produce a hearty, country texture, or processed until smooth and served with cream and snipped chives for a more luxurious soup.

Serves 4–6

4 tablespoons lightly salted butter
1 onion, chopped
3 leeks, sliced
2 potatoes, cut into $^3/_4$-inch cubes
$3^1/_2$ cups vegetable stock
salt and pepper
$^2/_3$ cup light cream (optional), to serve
2 tbsp snipped fresh chives, to garnish

❧ Melt the butter in a large saucepan over medium heat, add the prepared vegetables, and sauté gently for 2–3 minutes, until soft but not brown. Pour in the stock and bring to a boil, then reduce the heat and simmer, covered, for 15 minutes.

❧ Remove from the heat and blend the soup in the saucepan using a handheld immersion blender if you have one. Alternatively, pour into a blender or food processor, process until smooth, and return to the rinsed-out saucepan.

❧ Reheat the soup and season to taste with salt and pepper. Ladle into warm bowls and serve, swirled with the cream, if using, and garnished with the chives.

Beef & Barley Broth

In Irish cuisine, instead of a clear soup or stock, broth refers to a hearty meal-in-a-bowl soup. Traditionally, the meat is cut up and divided among individual soup bowls before the broth is poured over. A floury potato for mopping up juices tops each bowl.

Serves 6

1 1/2 pounds chuck steak
1/3 cup pearl barley, rinsed
1/3 cup green split peas, rinsed
1 large onion, thickly sliced
1/2 teaspoon black peppercorns
3 carrots, halved lengthwise and sliced
3/4 cup diced rutabaga or turnip
1 small leek, some green tops included,
   thinly sliced
1 celery stalk, sliced
6 small floury potatoes, such as russets,
   white rounders, or Yukon golds, peeled
1 1/2 cups sliced green cabbage
2 tablespoons chopped fresh parsley
salt

❈ Put the beef, pearl barley, and split peas in a large saucepan with the onion and peppercorns. Pour in enough cold water to just cover. Slowly bring to a boil, skimming off any foam, then reduce the heat, cover, and simmer gently for 1 1/2 hours.

❈ Add the carrots, rutabaga, leek, and celery to the pan. Season with salt, and simmer for an additional 30 minutes. Add a little more water if the soup starts to look too thick.

❈ Meanwhile, put the potatoes in another saucepan with water to cover. Add salt to taste and bring to a boil. Cook for 7–10 minutes, until tender but not disintegrating. Drain, return to the pan, and cover with a clean dish towel.

❈ Remove the meat saucepan from the stove. Carefully lift out the meat using two forks or a slotted spoon. Cut into small cubes and return to the pan. Add the cabbage and simmer for an additional 5 minutes, or until the cabbage is just tender. Check the seasoning.

❈ Ladle the soup into warm wide soup bowls. Place a potato in the middle of each bowl and sprinkle with the parsley.

Smoked Cod Chowder

With its hundreds of miles of coastline, it is no wonder that Ireland is famous for its fabulous fish and seafood. This recipe uses smoked cod, which gives the chowder a wonderfully rich flavor.

Serves 4

2 tablespoons salted butter
1 onion, finely chopped
1 small celery stalk, finely diced
2 potatoes, diced
1 small carrot, diced
1¼ cups boiling water
12 ounces smoked cod fillets, skinned
  and cut into bite-size pieces
1¼ cups whole milk
salt and pepper
fresh flat-leaf parsley sprigs, to garnish

❖ Melt the butter in a large saucepan over low heat, add the onion and celery, and cook, stirring frequently, for 5 minutes, or until soft but not brown.

❖ Add the potatoes, carrots, water, and salt and pepper to taste. Bring to a boil, then reduce the heat and simmer for 10 minutes, or until the vegetables are tender. Add the fish to the chowder and cook for an additional 10 minutes.

❖ Pour in the milk and heat gently. Taste and adjust the seasoning, adding salt and pepper if necessary. Ladle into warm bowls and serve garnished with parsley sprigs.

MUSSENDEN TEMPLE, COUNTY DERRY

Scallop Chowder

Scallops are fished around the Irish coast, especially in winter and spring. With their dense flesh and delicately flavored corals, they are particularly good in creamy chowders, either on their own or mixed with other seafood. Be careful to avoid overcooking them, otherwise the flesh will become rubbery.

Serves 6

3¹/₂ tablespoons lightly salted butter
9 ounces large scallops, quartered
4 bacon strips, chopped
1 large onion, chopped
2 celery stalks, diced
2 carrots, diced
3 starchy potatoes, such as russets, white round, or Yukon gold, diced
2 fresh thyme sprigs
3 tablespoons chopped fresh parsley
2 cups chicken or vegetable stock
2 cups whole milk, scalded
9 ounces mixed cooked seafood, such as shrimp and mussels
squeeze of lemon juice
salt and pepper

❧ Melt the butter in a large saucepan over medium heat. When it sizzles, add the scallops and cook, in batches, for 5 minutes, until lightly colored. Remove from the pan and set aside.

❧ Add the bacon to the pan and cook for 3–4 minutes, until it starts to color.

❧ Add the onion, celery, carrots, and potatoes. Season with salt and pepper, then cover and cook over medium-low heat, stirring occasionally, until the vegetables start to soften.

❧ Add the thyme and 2 tablespoons of the parsley to the pan of vegetables. Pour in the stock, cover, and bring to a boil. Reduce the heat and simmer for 15 minutes, until the vegetables are soft.

❧ Remove and discard the thyme sprigs. Lightly crush some of the vegetables with a masher or the back of a wooden spoon to thicken the liquid. Pour in the scalded milk.

❧ Add the scallops and mixed seafood to the pan. Cook until heated through but without letting the mixture boil.

❧ Check the seasoning, and add a squeeze of lemon juice. Ladle into warm bowls and serve sprinkled with the remaining parsley.

Split Pea & Ham Soup

This heartwarming soup benefits from the long, slow cooking process used in this recipe. It is a great way to use up any leftover ham and is perfect on its own as a light lunch, or served with bread for a filling and satisfying main meal.

Serves 6–8

$2^1/_2$ cups split green peas
1 tablespoon olive oil
1 large onion, finely chopped
1 large carrot, finely chopped
1 celery stalk, finely chopped
$4^1/_4$ cups chicken or vegetable stock
$4^1/_4$ cups water
8 ounces lean smoked ham,
   finely diced
$^1/_4$ teaspoon dried thyme
$^1/_4$ teaspoon dried marjoram
1 bay leaf
salt and pepper

- Rinse the peas under cold running water. Put in a saucepan and cover generously with water. Bring to a boil and boil for 3 minutes, skimming off the foam from the surface. Drain the peas.

- Heat the oil in a large saucepan over medium heat. Add the onion and cook for 3–4 minutes, stirring occasionally, until just softened.

- Add the carrot and celery and continue cooking for 2 minutes. Add the peas, pour in the stock and water, and stir to combine.

- Bring just to a boil and stir the ham into the soup. Add the thyme, marjoram, and bay leaf. Reduce the heat, cover, and cook gently for 1–$1^1/_2$ hours, until the ingredients are soft. Remove and discard the bay leaf.

- Taste and adjust the seasoning, adding salt and pepper if necessary. Ladle into warm bowls and serve.

Skink Soup

"Skink" is an old Irish and Scots term meaning "broth." This version, sometimes called Irish chicken soup, is made with diced chicken and colorful summer vegetables, enriched with cream and egg yolk. Although lighter than traditional winter broths, it still makes a satisfying meal-in-a-bowl.

Serves 4

2 celery stalks, halved lengthwise and diced

4 small carrots, thinly sliced

1 small leek, halved lengthwise and sliced

3½ cups chicken stock

1 bay leaf

1 cup diced cooked chicken

½ cup shelled peas

4 small scallions, some green tops included, sliced

1 egg yolk

⅓ cup heavy whipping cream

4 Boston or butter lettuce leaves, shredded

salt and pepper

- Put the celery, carrots, and leek in a saucepan with the stock, bay leaf, and salt and pepper to taste. Cover and bring to a boil. Reduce the heat to medium, then simmer for 15 minutes, or until tender.

- Add the chicken, peas, and scallions. Simmer for about 8 minutes, or until the peas are just tender.

- Remove the pan from the heat. Lightly beat the egg yolk and cream together, and stir the mixture into the soup. Reheat gently, stirring.

- Ladle into warm bowls, add the lettuce, and serve immediately.

Rye Toast with Roast Beef & Coleslaw

Beef and cabbage is a classic and tasty combination, as demonstrated by this chunky beef sandwich with homemade coleslaw. You can use any leftover corned beef in place of the roast beef (see page 54).

Serves 1

1 tablespoon finely chopped fresh
   ginger, or horseradish sauce
1¹/₂ tablespoons salted butter, softened
2 slices light rye bread
1 thin slice of green or white cabbage
1 small carrot, coarsely grated
1 scallion, sliced
1 large slice of roast beef
salt and pepper
dill pickles, to serve (optional)

❋ Preheat the broiler to medium-high. Meanwhile, mix the ginger with the butter.

❋ Spread one slice of bread generously with some of the butter. Top with the cabbage, trimming any overhanging shreds and placing them back in the middle of the sandwich. Top with the carrot and scallion, keeping them away from the edge. Season lightly with salt and pepper.

❋ Spread a little more of the butter on one side of the beef and lay it, butter-side down, on the carrot. Spread the remaining butter on the second slice of bread and place it on top of the sandwich, butter side down.

❋ Toast the sandwich under the preheated broiler on both sides, until crisp and golden. Serve immediately with pickles, if using.

Irish Rarebit

Meaning "tasty morsel," "rarebit" (or "rabbit") is a popular light course throughout Ireland and the British Isles, where it is traditionally served at "high tea." Numerous recipes exist, but most include cheese and mustard. Rarebit is delicious on toasted Irish soda bread, topped with chopped pickles.

Serves 4

2 cups shredded mild cheddar cheese
2 tablespoons lightly salted butter
$1/4$ cup whole milk
1 teaspoon cider vinegar
1 teaspoon dry mustard
4 slices whole wheat or soda bread
2 tablespoons chopped dill pickles
salt and pepper

❇ Preheat the broiler until hot. Put the cheese, butter, and milk in a saucepan and heat gently, stirring, until creamy and smooth. Add the vinegar, mustard, and seasoning to the sauce.

❇ Toast the bread on only one side. Place on a baking sheet, uncooked side facing upward. Pour the sauce over the bread. Place under the preheated broiler for 2–3 minutes, until golden and bubbling.

❇ Sprinkle with the chopped pickles and serve immediately.

GLENOE VILLAGE, COUNTY ANTRIM

HIGH CROSSES (LEFT); RURAL ROAD, IRELAND (ABOVE)

Glazed Beet & Egg Sourdough Toasts

With its vibrant color and sweet flavor, beet looks just as good as it tastes. In this recipe, it is partnered by chopped boiled eggs to make a tasty toast topping. When cooking fresh beets, leave one inch of stem attached to prevent the color from bleeding and peel after cooking.

Serves 2–4

4 eggs
10 cooked beets
2 teaspoons sugar, or to taste
1½ tablespoons cider vinegar, or to taste
4 slices sourdough bread
⅓ cup olive oil
1 tablespoon Dijon mustard
3 tablespoons chopped fresh dill
salt and pepper

Preheat the broiler to medium-high. Cook the eggs in a saucepan of boiling water for 8 minutes, then drain, shell, and chop them. Set aside.

Cut the beets into small dice and place in a small bowl. Mix in half of the sugar and 1 teaspoon of the vinegar and season to taste with salt and pepper.

Brush the bread with a little of the oil and toast under the preheated broiler for 2–3 minutes, until crisp and golden.

Meanwhile, drizzle 1 teaspoon of the remaining oil over the beets. Whisk together the remaining vinegar and sugar with the mustard and salt and pepper to taste. Gradually whisk in the remaining oil to make a thick dressing. Stir in the dill and taste for seasoning—it should be sweet and mustardy, with a sharpness—add more sugar or vinegar if you like.

Turn the bread over and stir the beets. Top the bread with the beets, covering the slices right up to the crusts. Glaze the beets under the broiler for 2–3 minutes, until browned in places.

Cut the slices in half or quarters and top with the reserved chopped egg. Drizzle with a little dressing and serve immediately.

Smoked Mackerel & Horseradish Pâté

Mackerel is plentiful in Ireland and is a versatile fish, used either fresh, cured, or smoked. In this recipe, it is combined with horseradish in a tasty pâté. Fresh horseradish is in season from summer to early fall in Ireland, but in the United States it is available in fall or early spring. It is also available already grated in jars.

Serves 4

8 ounces smoked mackerel fillets
finely grated zest and juice of 1 lemon
½ cup cream cheese
¼ cup freshly grated horseradish or
   good-quality horseradish sauce
2 tablespoons chopped fresh parsley
½ teaspoon black pepper
½ teaspoon sea salt flakes
whole wheat toast, to serve

❧ Remove the skin and any bones from the mackerel fillets and flake the flesh.

❧ Mix the fish with the lemon zest and juice, the cream cheese, and horseradish. Mash to a spreadable consistency, then add the parsley, pepper, and sea salt. Chill until ready to serve.

❧ Serve with hot whole wheat toast.

CLIFFS OF MOHER, COUNTY CLARE

Pickled Herring, Apple & Celery Salad

Herrings have always been abundant in Ireland. In this recipe, they are tossed with potatoes, crisp apples, and celery in a creamy dill-flavored dressing. If you have not eaten herring before, this is a good recipe for trying the fish for the first time.

Serves 4

8 small waxy potatoes, such as red-
   skinned new potatoes, unpeeled
6 pickled herring fillets, about
   10 ounces in total
2 red, crisp apples, unpeeled
lemon juice, for sprinkling
4 celery stalks, with leaves
2 pickles, sliced
1 romaine lettuce heart
salt and pepper

Dressing
1/2 cup sour cream or crème fraîche
1 tablespoon cider vinegar or white
   wine vinegar
1/2 teaspoon dry mustard
2 tablespoons chopped fresh dill
1 tablespoon olive oil
pinch of sugar
salt and pepper

❖ Put the unpeeled potatoes in a saucepan of salted water. Bring to a boil, then boil for about 10 minutes, or until just tender. Drain and spread out on a clean dish towel to dry. Slice thickly and set aside until cool.

❖ Meanwhile, make the dressing. Combine all the ingredients in a bowl and whisk until smooth.

❖ Cut the herring fillets into bite-size pieces. Quarter and core the apples, then slice into segments. Sprinkle the apple slices with a little lemon juice to prevent discoloration. Cut off and reserve the celery leaves, then quarter the celery stalks lengthwise and slice widthwise into 2³⁄₄-inch sticks.

❖ Put the herrings, apples, and celery in a large bowl with the sliced potatoes and pickles. Season to taste with salt and pepper and toss gently to mix.

❖ Remove the stems from the lettuce leaves, tear the leaves into large pieces, and arrange them on individual serving plates. Pile the herring mixture on top and spoon over the dressing. Garnish with the reserved celery leaves and serve immediately.

Garlic & Herb Dublin Bay Prawns

Dublin Bay prawns are part of the lobster family. Fresh Dublin Bay prawns are available outside Ireland, but if you can't find them you can use fresh spiny lobster, crayfish, or jumbo shrimp instead—the lobster is larger, but the crayfish and shrimp are smaller. This dish is delicious served with a glass of chilled white wine.

Serves 2

12 fresh Dublin Bay prawns in
  their shells
juice of 1/2 lemon
2 garlic cloves, crushed
3 tablespoons chopped fresh parsley
1 tablespoon chopped fresh dill
3 tablespoons salted butter, softened
salt and pepper
lemon wedges and crusty bread,
  to serve

❖ Rinse the prawns. Devein, using a sharp knife to slice along the back from the head end to the tail and removing the thin black intestine.

❖ Mix the lemon juice with the garlic, herbs, and butter to form a paste. Season well with salt and pepper. Spread the paste over the prawns and let marinate for 30 minutes. Meanwhile, preheat the broiler to medium.

❖ Cook the prawns under the preheated broiler for 5–6 minutes. Alternatively, heat a skillet and cook the prawns until cooked through. Turn out onto warm plates and pour over the pan juices. Serve immediately with lemon wedges and crusty bread.

ROCK OF CASHEL, COUNTY TIPPERARY

Irish Seafood Cocktail

Based on the traditional shrimp cocktail, this dish makes the most of Ireland's bountiful seafood. Crab, shrimp, and large meaty prawns are used in this recipe, but any combination will do. It's important that the seafood is particularly fresh.

Serves 4

4 crisp lettuce leaves, shredded
4-inch piece cucumber
1 cup white crabmeat
1 cup shelled, cooked shrimp
12 large, headless, cooked prawns or crayfish with shells
sea salt flakes
lemon slices
paprika, a few pinches

Cocktail sauce
$2/3$ cup good-quality mayonnaise
2 tablespoons ketchup
$1/2$ teaspoon Cognac
$1/4$ teaspoon Tabasco sauce

¤ To make the cocktail sauce combine all the ingredients in a pitcher, mixing well.

¤ Divide the lettuce among four cocktail glasses or ceramic bowls.

¤ Remove alternate strips of peel from the cucumber, and quarter the flesh lengthwise. Cut three of the pieces into small dice and sprinkle on top of the lettuce. Slice the remaining piece lengthwise into four sticks and set aside.

¤ Layer the crabmeat and shrimp on top of the cucumber. Season with crumbled sea salt flakes.

¤ Remove the shells from eight of the prawns. Arrange the shelled prawns on top of the crabmeat and shrimp. Season with a little more salt, then pour the sauce over the top.

¤ Garnish with the unshelled prawns, reserved cucumber sticks, and the lemon slices. Sprinkle with a pinch of paprika and serve.

Potted Crab

"Potting" is a method from pre-refrigeration days for preserving all kinds of meat and fish. More recently, it has become a way of stretching extravagant ingredients a little farther. The food is packed into small pots and covered with a layer of melted butter or other fat to exclude the air.

Serves 4–6

1 large cooked crab, prepared by your fish dealer if possible
whole nutmeg, for grating
2 pinches of cayenne pepper or mace
juice of 1 lemon
1 cup (2 sticks) lightly salted butter
salt and pepper
buttered toast, to serve

➐ If the crab is not already prepared, pick out all the meat, being particularly careful to remove all the meat from the claws.

➐ Mix together the white and brown crabmeat but do not mash too smoothly. Season well with salt and pepper and add a good grating of nutmeg and the cayenne pepper. Add the lemon juice to taste.

➐ Melt half of the butter in a saucepan and carefully mix in the crabmeat. Transfer the mixture into 4–6 small soufflé dishes or ramekins (individual ceramic dishes).

➐ In a clean saucepan, heat the remaining butter until it melts, then continue heating for a few moments until it stops bubbling. Let the sediment settle and carefully pour the clarified butter over the crab mixture. This seal of clarified butter lets you keep the potted crab for 1–2 days. Chill in the refrigerator for 1–2 hours.

➐ Serve with buttered toast.

Smoked Salmon, Dill & Horseradish Tartlets

Salmon has been smoked in Ireland for many centuries using traditional smoking techniques that capture and enhance both the flavor and texture of this fantastic fish. If you're short of time, you can use store-bought pastry dough instead of making it fresh.

Makes 6

Pastry dough
1 cup all-purpose flour, plus extra
   for dusting
pinch of salt
5½ tablespoons cold salted butter, cut
   into pieces, plus extra for greasing

Filling
½ cup crème fraîche, or ¼ cup sour
   cream mixed with ¼ cup heavy cream
1 teaspoon creamed horseradish
½ teaspoon lemon juice
1 teaspoon capers, chopped
3 egg yolks
8 ounces smoked salmon trimmings
bunch of fresh dill, chopped, plus extra
   sprigs to garnish
salt and pepper

❖ Grease six 3½-inch loose-bottom fluted tart pans. Sift the flour and salt into a food processor, add the butter, and process until the mixture resembles fine bread crumbs. Transfer the mixture to a large bowl and add just enough cold water to bring the dough together.

❖ Turn out onto a floured surface and divide into six equal pieces. Roll out each dough piece to a circle to fit the tart pans. Carefully fit each dough circle into a tart pan, pressing it to fit well. Roll the rolling pin over the pan to neaten the edges and trim the excess dough. Put a piece of parchment paper in each pan, fill with pie weights or dried beans, and chill in the refrigerator for 30 minutes. Meanwhile, preheat the oven to 400°F.

❖ Bake the pastry shells in the preheated oven for 10 minutes, then carefully remove the paper and weights.

❖ Meanwhile, to make the filling, put the crème fraîche, horseradish, lemon juice, and capers into a bowl with salt and pepper to taste and mix well. Add the egg yolks, smoked salmon, and chopped dill and carefully mix again. Divide this mixture among the pastry shells and return to the oven for 10 minutes. Let cool in the pans for 5 minutes before serving, garnished with dill sprigs.

Kipper & Potato Salad with Mustard Dressing

Made with gutted and split herrings smoked over oak chips, kippers are one of Ireland's best-loved cured fish. Their tasty dense, brown flesh is excellent eaten raw in a salad, as in this recipe, but it is also good broiled or briefly boiled in water.

Serves 4–6

1½ pounds waxy new potatoes, scrubbed
3 tablespoons chopped fresh dill, plus sprigs to garnish
4 scallions, some green tops included, diagonally sliced
8 radishes, sliced
4 kipper fillets, about 2½ ounces each
salt

Mustard dressing
1 teaspoon dry mustard
pinch of sugar
salt and pepper
2 tablespoons cider vinegar
2 tablespoons heavy cream
3 tablespoons peanut oil
3 tablespoons olive oil

❧ Cook the potatoes in boiling salted water for 15–20 minutes, or until just tender. Drain and slice widthwise into ¼-inch pieces. Set aside to cool.

❧ To make the dressing, combine the mustard, sugar, salt and pepper, cider vinegar, and heavy cream. Gradually add the oils, whisking until smooth and thick.

❧ Put the potatoes in a bowl, and mix with the dressing and dill. Add most of the scallions and radishes, reserving a few to garnish. Check the seasoning, and add more salt and pepper if necessary.

❧ Remove the skin from the kipper fillets. Slice each fillet lengthwise into four, then slice each piece widthwise into thin bite-size strips.

❧ Divide the potato mixture among individual serving plates. Arrange the kipper strips attractively on top, and garnish with the reserved scallions, radishes, and dill sprigs.

Blue Cheese &
Walnut Tartlets

So lush and green are the pasturelands that Irish dairy herds graze upon that it is no surprise that the resulting cheeses are of equally fine quality. Try using an Irish blue cheese, such as Cashel Blue, to make these tarts. Many Irish cheeses are available worldwide in supermarkets and specialty stores.

Makes 12

Pastry dough
1³/₄ cups all-purpose flour, plus extra
   for dusting
pinch of celery salt
7 tablespoons cold lightly salted butter,
   cut into pieces, plus extra for greasing
¹/₄ cup finely chopped walnut halves

Filling
2 tablespoons lightly salted butter
2 celery stalks, trimmed and
   finely chopped
1 small leek, trimmed and
   finely chopped
8 ounces blue cheese
1 cup heavy cream
3 egg yolks
salt and pepper

❧ Lightly grease twelve 3-inch cups in a muffin pan. Sift the flour and celery salt into a food processor, add the butter, and process until the mixture resembles fine bread crumbs. Transfer the mixture to a large bowl and add the walnuts and just enough cold water to bring the dough together.

❧ Turn out onto a floured surface and cut the dough in half. Roll out the first piece and cut out six 3¹/₂-inch circles. Take each circle and roll out to 4¹/₂ inches in diameter and fit into the muffin pan, pressing to fill the hole. Do the same with the remaining dough. Put a piece of parchment paper in each hole and fill with pie weights or dried beans, then let chill in the refrigerator for 30 minutes. Meanwhile, preheat the oven to 400°F.

❧ Remove the muffin pan from the refrigerator and bake the tarts in the preheated oven for 10 minutes, then carefully remove the paper and weights.

❧ Meanwhile, make the filling. Melt the butter in a skillet, add the celery and leek, and cook for 15 minutes, until soft. Add 2 tablespoons of the cream and crumble in the cheese, then mix well and season to taste with salt and pepper. Bring the remaining cream to a simmer in a separate saucepan, put the egg yolks into a heatproof bowl and pour the cream on to them, stirring all the time. Mix in the cheese mixture and spoon into the pastry shells. Bake for 10 minutes, then turn the pan around in the oven and bake for an additional 5 minutes. Let cool in the pan for 5 minutes before serving.

Bacon, Beet & Spinach Salad with Cashel Blue Cheese

Cashel Blue cheese is made near the Rock of Cashel in County Tipperary. When mature, it develops a mellow, slightly spicy flavor that goes well with beets. A good alternative would be a traditional farmhouse hard blue cheese such as Maytag Blue.

Serves 4–6

10–12 small beets, no more than
  2 inches in diameter
6 bacon strips
4 cups baby spinach
6 ounces Cashel Blue cheese, broken
  into small chunks
1/3 cup toasted hazelnuts
2 tablespoons chopped chives

Dressing
1 shallot, finely chopped
2 teaspoons white wine vinegar
1 teaspoon Dijon mustard
salt and pepper
1/3 cup extra virgin olive oil

❖ Preheat the broiler to high. Trim all but ½ inch of stem from the beets and any long roots. Leave the peel in place. Plunge into a large saucepan of boiling water, bring back to a boil, then simmer briskly for about 30 minutes, or until the beets are just tender. Drain and let cool a little.

❖ Meanwhile, broil the bacon for 4–5 minutes, turning once, until crisp. Blot with paper towels and slice widthwise into bite-size pieces. Set aside and keep warm.

❖ Whisk together the dressing ingredients in a pitcher and set aside.

❖ When the beets are cool enough to handle, remove the peel, leaving the stem in place and being careful to avoid damaging the flesh. Using a sharp knife, slice the beets in half lengthwise.

❖ Arrange the spinach leaves on a serving platter or individual plates. Whisk the dressing again and spoon a little over the leaves. Arrange the beets attractively on top and pour the remaining dressing over them. Scatter with the cheese, bacon, and nuts, finishing with a sprinkling of chives.

Chapter 2
ENTRÉES

Sea Trout with Cider & Cream Sauce

With its extensive coastline and rivers, Ireland boasts an abundance of sea trout and salmon. Here, a whole fish is cooked in foil with typically Irish flavorings—cider and leeks—which add depth of flavor to the cream sauce. The dish makes a splendid centerpiece for a special occasion.

Serves 8–10

7¾-pound whole sea trout or salmon, gutted

oil, for brushing

small bunch parsley, plus a few extra sprigs to garnish

2 fresh bay leaves

sea salt flakes

black pepper

1 leek, halved lengthwise and sliced

2 lemons, thinly sliced

3½ tablespoons lightly salted butter

1 cup dry hard cider

1 cup light cream

3 tablespoons chopped fresh tarragon or dill

boiled new potatoes and peas, to serve

❧ Preheat the oven to 350°F. Line a roasting pan with thick aluminum foil large enough to loosely enclose the fish in a sealed package. Brush the inside of the foil with oil.

❧ Remove the head, tail, and fins from the fish. Place the fish on the foil and stuff the cavity with the parsley and bay leaves. Rub all over with sea salt flakes and black pepper. Arrange the leek slices and half of the lemon slices over the fish, and dot with the butter. Gather up the foil and pour the cider around the fish. Seal the foil well, leaving a small vent at the top.

❧ Place the fish package in the roasting pan in the preheated oven and bake for 1¼ hours, or until the thickest part of the flesh looks opaque when pierced with the tip of a knife. Open the foil and carefully slide the fish onto a warm serving platter, discarding the parsley, bay leaves, lemon, and leek. Keep warm.

❧ Transfer the juices from the foil into the pan, along with any that flow from the fish, and place on the stove over medium-high heat. Stir in the cream and tarragon, then simmer briskly for 10–15 minutes, until slightly thickened. Check the seasoning and pour into a pitcher.

❧ Remove the skin from the top of the fish. Garnish with the remaining lemon slices and parsley sprigs. Serve with the sauce, new potatoes, and peas.

Corned Beef & Cabbage

This dish is traditionally eaten in the United States to celebrate Saint Patrick's Day. In the past, the brining liquid may have included saltpeter, a bactericide that also produces the characteristic color. Saltpeter is no longer available to the general public, but you may be able to buy brine mix from a good butcher.

Serves 6–8

3½ quarts water
1½ pounds coarse salt or brine mix
3¼-pound brisket, bottom round roast, or rump roast
12 black peppercorns
4 cloves
3 bay leaves
1 large onion, sliced
6 carrots, cut into chunks
1 turnip, thickly sliced
6 large potatoes, cut into chunks
1 savoy or green cabbage, cored and cut into wedges
2 tablespoons chopped fresh parsley
mustard, to serve

❧ Pour the water into a large plastic or ceramic container and chill in the refrigerator for 1 hour. Stir in the salt until it has dissolved completely, then add the meat, making sure that it is completely submerged.

❧ Put the container in the refrigerator for 7–10 days. Check daily that the meat is still submerged and skim off any foam that rises to the surface.

❧ Drain the meat, discarding the soaking liquid, then rinse. Put the meat into a large saucepan, add the peppercorns, cloves, and bay leaves, and pour in enough water to cover. Bring to a boil, skimming off any foam that rises to the surface. Reduce the heat, cover, and simmer gently for 1¾ hours.

❧ Add the onion, carrots, turnip, and potatoes to the pan, re-cover, and simmer for 30 minutes. Add the cabbage and parsley, re-cover, and simmer for an additional 15–30 minutes, until the meat is tender.

❧ Remove the beef, cover with aluminum foil, and let rest for 10 minutes, until firm. Strain the vegetables and put them into a warm serving dish, discarding the peppercorns, cloves, and bay leaves. Carve the meat into slices and serve immediately with the vegetables and mustard.

Cockle & Mussel Gratin

Cockles and mussels have always been popular in Irish coastal communities. They could be collected from the shore instead of risking the potential peril of a boat. In this recipe, the two are cooked in a rich and tasty gratin. The crisp topping provides contrasting texture and flavor to the seafood below. If you can't find cockles, use small clams instead.

Serves 3–4

1³/₄ pounds mussels
¹/₂ cup water
¹/₂ cup (1 stick) lightly salted butter
2 onions, chopped
1¹/₄ cups cooked shelled cockles
juice and finely grated zest of ¹/₂ lemon
3 tablespoons chopped fresh parsley
salt and pepper
1 cup coarse bread crumbs from
  a day-old ciabatta loaf
2 garlic cloves, finely chopped

- ❀ Preheat the oven to 425°F. Scrub and beard the mussels, discarding any with broken shells or that remain open. Put in a large saucepan with the water. Cover and steam for 4–5 minutes, until the shells open. Discard any that remain closed. Reserve eight mussels in their shells as a garnish. Remove the rest from the shells.

- ❀ Melt half of the butter in a skillet over medium-high heat. Add the onions and sauté for 7 minutes, until soft but not colored. Transfer to a 2-quart gratin dish.

- ❀ Add the cockles, shelled mussels, lemon juice, and 2 tablespoons of the parsley. Season with salt and pepper and stir to mix.

- ❀ Set aside a pat of butter and melt the remaining butter. Mix with the bread crumbs, garlic, lemon zest, and remaining parsley. Season with a little more salt and pepper.

- ❀ Spread the bread-crumb mixture over the seafood. Top with the reserved mussels and dot them with the remaining butter.

- ❀ Bake in the oven for 10–15 minutes, until the crumbs are golden and crisp and the seafood is thoroughly heated. Serve immediately.

# Beef in Stout with Herb Dumplings

Stout is a strong, dark beer that originated in the British Isles. The most famous Irish stout is Guinness, which is made from roasted, malted barley, hops, yeast, and water. In this hearty stew, topped with light and fluffy suet dumplings, tender chunks of slow-cooked beef are enveloped in a rich gravy.

Serves 6

2 tablespoons sunflower oil
2 large onions, thinly sliced
8 carrots, sliced
1/4 cup all-purpose flour
2 3/4 pounds chuck short ribs or center
   cut beef shanks, cut into cubes
2 cups stout
2 teaspoons firmly packed
   dark brown sugar
2 bay leaves
1 tablespoon chopped fresh thyme
salt and pepper

Herb dumplings
1 cup all-purpose flour
1 1/2 teaspoons baking powder
1/2 teaspoon salt
1/4 cup shredded suet (available from
   butchers) or shortening
2 tablespoons chopped fresh parsley,
   plus extra to garnish
about 1/4 cup water

Preheat the oven to 325°F. Heat the oil in a flameproof casserole dish. Add the onions and carrots and cook over low heat, stirring occasionally, for 5 minutes, or until the onions are softened. Meanwhile, put the flour in a plastic bag and season well with salt and pepper. Add the beef to the bag, tie the top, and shake well to coat. Do this in batches if necessary. Reserve any remaining seasoned flour.

Remove the onions and carrots from the casserole dish with a slotted spoon and reserve. Add the beef to the dish, in batches, and cook, stirring frequently, until browned all over. Return all the meat and the onions and carrots to the casserole dish and sprinkle in the reserved seasoned flour. Pour in the stout and add the sugar, bay leaves, and thyme. Bring to a boil, cover, and cook in the preheated oven for 1 3/4 hours.

To make the herb dumplings, sift the flour, baking powder, and salt into a bowl. Stir in the suet and parsley and add enough of the water to make a soft dough. Shape into small balls between the palms of your hands. Add to the casserole dish and return to the oven for 30 minutes. Remove and discard the bay leaves. Serve immediately, sprinkled with parsley.

Irish Stew

This robust stew was traditionally made using lamb or mutton (meat from a sheep over a year old), potatoes, onions, and sometimes carrots. It is a white stew, meaning that the meat is not browned. If you can, make it a day in advance so that the delicious flavors have time to blend together.

Serves 4

¼ cup all-purpose flour
3 pounds neck of lamb, trimmed of visible fat
3 large onions, chopped
3 carrots, sliced
4 starchy potatoes, such as russets, white round, or Yukon gold, quartered
½ teaspoon dried thyme
3½ cups hot beef stock
salt and pepper
2 tablespoons chopped fresh parsley, to garnish

❧ Preheat the oven to 325°F. Put the flour in a plastic bag and season well with salt and pepper. Add the lamb to the bag, tie the top, and shake well to coat. Do this in batches if necessary. Arrange the lamb in the bottom of a casserole dish.

❧ Layer the onions, carrots, and potatoes on top of the lamb.

❧ Sprinkle in the thyme and pour in the stock, then cover and cook in the preheated oven for 2½ hours. Garnish with the parsley and serve straight from the casserole dish.

COBH HARBOR, COUNTY CORK

Dublin Lawyer

A luxurious dish for two, Dublin Lawyer is reputedly named after the city's wealthy lawyers and their liking for large amounts of whiskey. The dish is usually made with lobster, which is plentiful in Ireland. This version with crab is just as delicious.

Serves 2

2 large cooked crabs
2 tablespoons lightly salted butter
1 shallot, finely chopped
1/4 cup Irish whiskey
1/2 cup heavy cream
sea salt flakes
black pepper
pinch of cayenne pepper
pinch of paprika, to garnish (optional)

To serve
steamed baby carrots
steamed sea asparagus or peas

• Pull the claws and legs from the crabs and separate at the joints into sections. Crack with a mallet. Use a skewer or teaspoon to pick out the meat from all the sections except the claws. Set these aside. Pick out the meat from the body section, discarding the pointed gills (dead men's fingers), the stomach sac, and any sludgy brown sediment.

• Melt the butter in a skillet over medium heat. Add the shallot and cook for 5 minutes, until soft. Add the crabmeat and the reserved cracked claws.

• Pour in the whiskey and ignite it. When the flames die down, stir in the cream. Season with sea salt, black pepper, and a pinch of cayenne. Stir for a few minutes until heated through.

• Divide between two warm plates. Garnish with a pinch of paprika, if using. Serve with lightly cooked baby carrots and sea asparagus or peas. Use your fingers to extract the crabmeat from the claws.

GEORGIAN DOORWAY, DUBLIN (LEFT); TRINITY COLLEGE, DUBLIN (ABOVE)

Pot-Roast Pork

Pork has long been a popular meat in Ireland. In this tasty
dish, pork tenderloin is slowly braised in hard cider and stock.
The resulting cooking liquid is then enriched with cream to
create a delicious sauce.

Serves 4

1 tablespoon sunflower oil
4 tablespoons lightly salted butter
2¼-pound boned and rolled
   pork tenderloin
4 shallots, chopped
6 juniper berries (optional)
2 fresh thyme sprigs, plus extra
   to garnish
²/₃ cup hard dry cider
²/₃ cup chicken stock or water
8 celery stalks, chopped
2 tablespoons all-purpose flour
²/₃ cup heavy cream
salt and pepper
freshly cooked peas, to serve

❖ Heat the oil with half of the butter in a heavy saucepan or
flameproof casserole dish. Add the pork and cook over medium
heat, turning frequently, for 5–10 minutes, or until browned.
Transfer to a plate.

❖ Add the shallots to the saucepan and cook, stirring frequently,
for 5 minutes, or until softened. Add the juniper berries, if using,
and thyme sprigs and return the pork to the saucepan with
any juices that have collected on the plate. Pour in the cider
and stock, season to taste with salt and pepper, then cover and
simmer for 30 minutes. Turn the pork over and add the celery.
Re-cover the pan and cook for an additional 40 minutes.

❖ Meanwhile, make a paste by mashing the remaining butter with
the flour in a small bowl. Transfer the pork and celery to a platter
with a slotted spoon and keep warm. Remove and discard the
juniper berries and thyme. Whisk the butter-and-flour paste, a
little at a time, into the simmering cooking liquid. Cook, stirring
continuously, for 2 minutes, then stir in the cream and bring
to a boil.

❖ Slice the pork and spoon a little of the sauce over it. Garnish with
thyme sprigs and serve immediately with the celery, peas, and the
remaining sauce.

Dublin Coddle

This nourishing and economical dish of bacon, sausage, and potatoes has been a favorite in Ireland, particularly in Dublin, since the seventeenth century. It is invariably served with soda bread to mop up the juices, which, if the dish has been properly "coddled," or slow-cooked, should be thick.

Serves 4–6

1 pound bacon strips
8 good-quality pork sausages
4 onions, sliced
black pepper
1 leek, some green tops included, sliced
2 bay leaves
2 sprigs thyme
1/4 cup chopped fresh parsley
2 garlic cloves, chopped
6 starchy potatoes, such as russets, peeled and cut into 2 or 3 large chunks
3 cups ham stock or chicken stock
soda bread, to serve

❖ Preheat the broiler to high and preheat the oven to 300°F. Broil the bacon for 7–8 minutes, until just starting to crisp. Drain on paper towels, slice in half widthwise, and set aside. Reserve the fat in the broiler pan.

❖ Heat a skillet over medium heat, add the sausages, and cook, turning, for about 15 minutes, until evenly browned. If necessary, use a little bacon fat to prevent the sausages from sticking. Remove the sausages from the skillet, slice in half widthwise, and set aside.

❖ Using the sausage skillet, gently cook the onions for 7 minutes, until soft but not colored. Add more bacon fat if necessary.

❖ Layer the onions, sausages, and bacon in the bottom of a flameproof casserole dish, seasoning each layer with plenty of black pepper. Add the leek, herbs, and garlic, and finish with a layer of potatoes. Season with a little more black pepper, then pour in the stock.

❖ Cover the casserole dish tightly and bring to a boil on top of the stove. Transfer to the preheated oven and cook for 45 minutes, or until the potatoes are tender.

❖ Serve with chunks of soda bread to mop up the juices.

Potato, Leek & Chicken Pie

The humble pie is a mainstay of Irish cuisine, being as versatile as it is delicious. This modern take on the traditional chicken and leek pie uses phyllo pastry to give it a crispy topping. Unlike many pies, it is the perfect dish for a summer day because it is light and not at all heavy.

Serves 4

2 waxy potatoes, such as russets, cubed
7 tablespoons lightly salted butter
1 skinless, boneless chicken breast,
  about 6 ounces, cubed
1 leek, sliced
2 cups sliced cremini mushrooms
2¹/₂ tablespoons all-purpose flour
1¹/₄ cups milk
1 tablespoon Dijon mustard
2 tablespoons chopped fresh sage
8 ounces phyllo pastry, thawed if frozen
salt and pepper

❧ Preheat the oven to 350°F. Cook the potatoes in a saucepan of boiling water for 5 minutes. Drain and set aside.

❧ Melt half of the butter in a skillet and cook the chicken for 5 minutes, or until browned all over.

❧ Add the leek and mushrooms and cook for 3 minutes, stirring. Stir in the flour and cook for 1 minute, stirring continuously. Gradually stir in the milk and bring to a boil. Add the mustard, sage, and potatoes, season to taste with salt and pepper, and simmer for 10 minutes.

❧ Meanwhile, melt the remaining butter in a small saucepan. Line a deep pie dish with half of the sheets of phyllo pastry. Spoon the chicken mixture into the dish and cover with a sheet of pastry. Brush the pastry with a little of the melted butter and lay another sheet on top. Brush this sheet with melted butter.

❧ Cut the remaining phyllo pastry into strips and fold them onto the top of the pie to create a ruffled effect. Brush the strips with the remaining melted butter and cook in the preheated oven for 45 minutes, or until golden brown and crisp. Serve hot.

Pork Tenderloin with Roasted Rhubarb

The pig has always been important in Ireland, and pork, either fresh or cured, features strongly in the cuisine. In this recipe, young pink rhubarb tempers the meat's natural sweetness and produces deliciously tangy juices. Use a blade-end or center-cut joint for moistness and flavor.

Serves 4

1³/₄-pound boneless pork tenderloin
olive oil
1 teaspoon sea salt flakes
¹/₂ teaspoon black pepper
10 small sprigs of rosemary
¹/₂ cup chicken stock
3¹/₂ pink rhubarb stalks, trimmed and
    diagonally sliced into 1¹/₂-inch lengths
1 tablespoon honey

❧ Preheat the oven to 375°F. Using the tip of a sharp knife, score the fat, but not the flesh, of the pork at ¹/₂-inch intervals. Tie the meat with kitchen twine to form a neat roll. You can ask your butcher to do both of these.

❧ Place the meat in a small roasting pan. Rub with oil, and then with the sea salt and black pepper, rubbing them in well. Insert the rosemary sprigs into the slits in the fat. Roast in the preheated oven for 40 minutes.

❧ Pour in the stock. Arrange the rhubarb around the meat and drizzle with the honey. Roast for another 10–15 minutes, until the rhubarb is tender and starting to color at the edges.

❧ Transfer the pork and rhubarb to a warm serving platter, reserving the pan juices. Make a tent over the meat with aluminum foil, and let rest for 10 minutes in a warm place.

❧ Place the roasting pan on the stove over medium-high heat. Let bubble rapidly to reduce the pan juices, including any that have flowed from the meat, for 3–4 minutes, until slightly thickened. Check the seasoning, strain into a pitcher, and serve with the meat.

Fisherman's Pie

Fish pie is a popular everyday comfort food, and it can be an excellent dish when made with good-quality, fresh ingredients. The rich, creamy sauce and the addition of shrimp and fresh herbs add to the luxury feeling, making this a dish worthy to grace any table.

Serves 6

2 pounds white fish fillets,
  such as flounder or sole, skinned
²/₃ cup dry white wine
1 tablespoon chopped fresh parsley,
  tarragon, or dill
2¹/₂ cups sliced white button
  mushrooms
7 tablespoons lightly salted butter,
  plus extra for greasing
6 ounces cooked, peeled shrimp
¹/₃ cup all-purpose flour
¹/₂ cup heavy cream
2 pounds starchy potatoes, such as
  russets or Yukon gold, cut into chunks
salt and pepper

- Preheat the oven to 350°F. Grease a 2-quart baking dish.

- Fold the fish fillets in half and place in the dish. Season well with salt and pepper, pour over the wine, and scatter over the herbs.

- Cover with aluminum foil and bake in the preheated oven for 15 minutes, until the fish starts to flake. Strain off the liquid and reserve for the sauce. Increase the oven temperature to 425°F.

- Heat 1 tablespoon of the butter in a skillet, add the mushrooms, and sauté them for about 5 minutes, or until they are soft and release their juices. Spoon them over the fish, then scatter the shrimp on top

- Heat 4 tablespoons of the remaining butter in a saucepan and stir in the flour. Cook for a few minutes without browning, then remove from the heat and add the reserved cooking liquid gradually, stirring well between each addition.

- Return the pan to the heat and gently bring to a boil, stirring. Add the cream and season to taste with salt and pepper. Pour the sauce over the fish in the dish and smooth over the surface.

- Meanwhile, cook the potatoes in a large saucepan of boiling salted water for 15–20 minutes. Drain well and mash with a potato masher until smooth. Season to taste with salt and pepper and add the remaining butter, stirring until melted.

- Pile or pipe the mashed potato onto the fish and sauce and bake in the preheated oven for 10–15 minutes, until golden brown.

Ham with Parsley Sauce

This is a comforting dish still worthy of serving at dinnertime. Make sure the steaks are "green" (the term used for unsmoked fresh ham), because smoked ham is too salty. Cut the steaks thick, otherwise the meat will dry out during cooking. Buy a small, boneless ham joint and slice it into steaks yourself.

Serves 4

1³/₄-pound fresh ham, cut into four
  ³/₄-inch-thick steaks
vegetable oil, for brushing

Parsley sauce
2 tablespoons unsalted butter
1 shallot, finely chopped
3 tablespoons all-purpose flour
³/₄ cup ham or chicken stock
1 cup whole milk
¹/₃ cup chopped fresh parsley
squeeze of lemon juice
¹/₂ teaspoon dry mustard
salt and white pepper

:: First make the parsley sauce. Melt the butter in a skillet over medium–low heat. Add the shallot and cook for 2–3 minutes, until soft but not colored.

:: Remove the skillet from the heat and stir in the flour. Return to the heat and cook for 1 minute, stirring. Reduce the heat to low, and whisk in the stock and milk. Keep whisking until the sauce starts to bubble. Stir in the parsley, then add the lemon juice, mustard, pepper, and a pinch of salt. Simmer gently, stirring often, for 20 minutes.

:: Meanwhile, remove the rind, but not the fat, from the ham steaks. Slash the fat at ³/₄-inch intervals. Brush with oil on both sides.

:: Heat a ridged grill pan over high heat. Cook the steaks on one side for 5–6 minutes. Once they start to color on the underside, cover with a lid and reduce the heat to medium. Turn and cook the other side for 5 minutes, covered.

:: Place the steaks on warm serving plates, pour the sauce over them, and serve.

ROUNDSTONE HARBOUR, COUNTY GALWAY (LEFT); GREAT ARCH, PORTRUSH, COUNTY ANTRIM (ABOVE)

Fish Cakes

Homemade fish cakes are a popular offering in seaside pubs, and their flavor is in a completely different league to that of the bland frozen fish cakes you may have eaten as a child. You can vary the fish according to what is available—a mixture of two or three types of fish, such as turbot and salmon, works well.

Serves 4

4 starchy potatoes, such as russets or
    Yukon gold, cut into chunks
1 pound mixed fish fillets, such as cod,
    halibut, salmon, or turbot, skinned
2 tablespoons chopped fresh tarragon
grated rind of 1 lemon
2 tablespoons heavy cream
1 tablespoon all-purpose flour
1 egg, beaten
2½ cups bread crumbs, made from
    day-old white or whole wheat bread
¼ cup vegetable oil, for shallow-frying
salt and pepper
watercress and lemon wedges, to serve

- Cook the potatoes in a large saucepan of boiling salted water for 15–20 minutes. Drain well and mash with a potato masher until smooth.

- Put the fish in a skillet and just cover with water. Place over medium heat and bring to a boil, then reduce the heat, cover, and simmer gently for 5 minutes, until cooked.

- Remove from the heat and drain the fish onto a plate. When cool enough to handle, flake the fish into large chunks, making sure that there are no bones.

- Mix the potatoes with the fish, tarragon, lemon rind, and cream. Season well with salt and pepper and shape into four large patties or eight smaller ones.

- Dust the patties with flour and dip them into the beaten egg. Coat thoroughly in the bread crumbs. Place on a baking sheet and let chill in the refrigerator for at least 30 minutes.

- Heat the oil in the skillet and cook the patties over medium heat for 5 minutes on each side, turning them carefully using a spatula.

- Serve with the watercress, accompanied by lemon wedges for squeezing over the fish cakes.

Blood Sausage with Caramelized Pear and Cider

Made from boiled pig's blood bound with barley or other grain, the blood sausage, called "black pudding" in Ireland, is a heavy-duty sausage that evolved from the need to use every part of the pig. It is popular at breakfast time in Ireland, where it is currently undergoing something of a renaissance, and modern chefs are using it in a variety of novel ways.

Serves 4

3¹/₂ tablespoons lightly salted butter
3 firm pears, such as Bosc, peeled,
    cored, and quartered lengthwise
12 ounces blood sausage, thickly sliced
2 shallots, chopped
¹/₂ cup chicken stock
¹/₂ cup dry hard cider
sea salt flakes
black pepper
¹/₂ cup light cream
squeeze of lemon juice
3 tablespoons chopped fresh parsley

Heat half of the butter in a heavy skillet. When it sizzles, sauté the pear segments over medium-low heat for 10 minutes, turning, until caramelized at the edges. Remove from the skillet and keep warm.

Add the blood sausage slices to the skillet and cook for 3 minutes on each side side, turning them carefully so that they don't disintegrate. Set aside and keep warm.

Pour off the fat and wipe the skillet clean with paper towels. Heat the remaining butter in the skillet, add the shallots, and cook for 3–4 minutes, until softened.

Pour in the stock and cider, raise the heat, and bring to a boil. Reduce the heat a little, then simmer briskly for 5–7 minutes, until reduced by half. Season with sea salt and plenty of pepper.

Add the cream to the skillet and simmer for about a minute, until slightly thickened.

Return the pear slices to the skillet, add a squeeze of lemon, and cook for an additional minute, or until heated through. Sprinkle with the parsley and serve with the sausage slices.

Winter Vegetable Cobbler

While a cobbler can be a fruit dessert similar to a crisp, any cobbler dish found on the menu in an Irish pub is more likely to be a main course or side dish, not a dessert. Cobblers are typically meat stews topped with thick circles of a biscuit-like dough, with each circle forming a separate "cobble." This is a vegetarian version.

Serves 4

1 tbsp olive oil
1 garlic clove, crushed
8 small onions, halved
2 celery stalks, sliced
2 carrots, sliced
1³/₄ cups chopped rutabaga (if available)
¹/₂ small cauliflower, broken into florets
3 cups sliced mushrooms
1²/₃ cups of canned chopped tomatoes
¹/₄ cup red lentils
2 tablespoons cornstarch
3–4 tablespoons water
1¹/₄ cups vegetable stock
2 teaspoons Tabasco sauce
2 teaspoons chopped fresh oregano,
   plus extra sprigs to garnish

Cobbler topping

1³/₄ cups all-purpose flour
2¹/₂ teaspoons baking powder
1 teaspoon salt
4 tablespoons lightly salted butter
1 cup shredded sharp cheddar cheese
2 teaspoons chopped fresh oregano
1 egg, lightly beaten
²/₃ cup milk

❧ Preheat the oven to 350°F. Heat the oil in a large flameproof casserole dish over medium heat, add the garlic and onions, and cook for 5 minutes, until softened. Add the celery, carrots, rutabaga, and cauliflower, and cook for 2–3 minutes. Add the mushrooms, tomatoes, and lentils. Mix together the cornstarch and water and stir into the casserole with the stock, Tabasco, and chopped oregano.

❧ Cover the casserole dish, then transfer to the preheated oven and bake for 20 minutes.

❧ To make the cobbler topping, sift the flour, baking powder, and salt into a bowl. Rub in the butter, then stir in most of the cheese and the chopped oregano. Beat the egg with the milk and add enough of the mixture to the dry ingredients to make a soft dough. Knead lightly, roll out to a thickness of ¹/₂ inch and cut into 2-inch circles.

❧ Remove the dish from the oven and increase the temperature to 400°F. Arrange the dough circles around the edge of the dish, brush with the remaining egg and milk, and sprinkle with the reserved cheese. Cook for an additional 10–12 minutes, or until the topping is golden brown. Garnish with oregano sprigs and serve.

Beef & Stout Pies

The Irish love their main-course pies—hot, warm, or cold, eaten at home, in a restaurant, or outdoors. These individual puff-pastry pies are made with richly flavored meat stock and stout, usually Guinness, which the Irish claim is the only dark ale suitable for cooking beef.

Serves 4

3 tablespoons all-purpose flour
1 teaspoon salt
1/2 teaspoon black pepper
2 pounds boneless chuck steak
  or eye of round steak, cut into
  1-inch pieces
vegetable oil, for frying
1 1/4 cups meat stock
1 onion, coarsely chopped
8 ounces cremini mushrooms,
  stems discarded, caps quartered
1 tablespoon tomato paste
2 teaspoons chopped fresh thyme
1 cup stout
1 pound store-bought puff pastry
1 egg yolk, lightly beaten

- Combine the flour, salt, and pepper in a bowl, then toss the beef in the mixture until evenly coated.

- Heat 3 tablespoons of oil in a large skillet over medium-high heat. Cook the beef, in batches, and transfer to a flameproof casserole dish. Deglaze the skillet with 1/4 cup of stock, and add the liquid to the casserole dish.

- Heat another 1–2 tablespoons of oil in the skillet and cook the onion and mushrooms for 6–7 minutes, until soft. Add to the casserole dish with the tomato paste, thyme, stout, and remaining stock. Heat the casserole dish over medium-high heat, bring to a boil, then simmer gently with the lid slightly askew for 1 1/2 hours. Check the seasoning.

- Drain the meat mixture in a strainer set over a bowl, reserving the liquid. Let rest until cool.

- Preheat the oven to 425°F. Put a baking sheet in the oven to heat.

- Divide the meat mixture among four individual 1 3/4-cup pie plates with a flat rim or ovenproof bowls. Pour in enough of the liquid to not quite cover the filling. Dampen the rims of the pie plates.

- Cut the pastry into quarters. Roll out each piece to about 1 inch bigger than the pie plates. From each quarter, cut a 1/2-inch strip and press it onto a dampened rim. Brush with egg yolk, then drape the pastry quarter on top, covering the strip. Trim, crimp the edges with a fork, and make three slashes down the middle. Decorate the tops with shapes cut from the trimmings. Brush with the remaining egg yolk.

- Place the pies on the preheated baking sheet and bake in the preheated oven for 20 minutes. Reduce the heat to 400°F and bake for an additional 5 minutes.

Slow-Roasted Shoulder of Lamb with Herb Dumplings

Like many traditional Irish lamb dishes, this is nourishing and delicious and made with an economical cut. The meat is slow-roasted at low heat until almost falling off the bone. Light and fluffy herb-flavored dumplings mop up the flavorsome juices.

Serves 4–6

2 large carrots, cut into thin sticks
1 onion, sliced
3¼-pound bone-in shoulder of lamb
2–3 fresh bay leaves
1 sage sprig
small bunch parsley
salt and pepper
2½ cups meat stock

Herb-flavored dumplings
1 cup all-purpose flour
1 teaspoon baking powder
½ teaspoon salt
¼ teaspoon black pepper
1½ tablespoons finely chopped
  fresh parsley
1½ tablespoons finely chopped fresh
  mint or herb of your choice
2 tablespoons lightly salted butter
1 egg
2 tablespoons milk

- Preheat the oven to 450°F. Scatter the carrots and onion over the bottom of a roasting pan slightly larger than the meat. Place the meat on top, tucking the herbs underneath. Season with salt and pepper, then pour in enough stock to not quite cover the vegetables.

- Cover the pan with thick aluminum foil, sealing the edges well. Roast in the preheated oven for 20 minutes, then reduce the heat to 325°F and roast for an additional 3 hours.

- To make the dumplings, sift the flour, baking powder, and salt into a bowl. Mix in the black pepper and herbs. Rub in the butter until the mixture resembles coarse bread crumbs. Beat together the egg and milk in a pitcher, then stir into the flour mixture to make a soft, slightly sticky dough.

- With floured hands, divide the dough into 12 pieces and roll into balls. Drop into a large saucepan of boiling salted water. Partially cover and cook for 15 minutes. Using tongs, gently lift the dumplings into a colander and let drain for a few minutes. Transfer to a plate until needed.

- Just before the meat is ready, heat the remaining stock in a small saucepan. Remove the meat from the oven and open up the foil. Arrange the dumplings around the meat and pour in the hot stock. Reseal the foil and roast for another 15 minutes.

- Transfer the meat to a warm platter and discard the herbs. Arrange the dumplings and vegetables around the meat. Strain the juices into a pitcher and serve with the meat.

Roast Goose with Apple Stuffing & Cider Gravy

In days gone by, it was customary in Ireland to eat a young goose on Michaelmas Day (September 29). According to Irish folklore, doing so provided protection from financial hardship. Michaelmas also coincided with the apple harvest, hence the tradition of an apple-based stuffing, as in this recipe, and applesauce as an accompaniment.

Serves 4–5

1 x 8³/₄-pound goose, with the giblets
  (the neck, heart, and gizzard) and
  lumps of fat in the cavity reserved,
  and wing tips and leg tips cut off
  and reserved
1 onion, coarsely chopped
1 celery stalk, coarsely chopped
1 large carrot, coarsely chopped
handful of parsley
2–3 thyme sprigs
2 fresh bay leaves
¹/₂ teaspoon black peppercorns
2 small firm apples
1 cup hard dry cider
2 tablespoons apple cider vinegar
2 tablespoons all-purpose flour
salt and pepper

Apple stuffing
3 onions, chopped
4 unsmoked bacon strips, chopped
4 starchy potatoes, such as russets,
  peeled and cut into ¹/₂-inch dice
3 cooking apples, such as Granny Smith
  or Gravenstein, quartered, cored,
  peeled, and coarsely chopped
1¹/₂ tablespoons chopped fresh sage
1 tablespoon chopped fresh thyme
¹/₂ teaspoon sea salt
¹/₄ teaspoon black pepper
4 ounces goose liver, chopped
2 tablespoons chopped fresh parsley
finely grated zest of 1 lemon

❧ Prick the goose all over with a fork and place in a colander. Douse with plenty of boiling water, then pat dry with paper towels. Season inside the cavity with salt and pepper, and rub salt all over the skin. Let dry.

❧ To make the stuffing, heat a pat of goose fat in a skillet over medium heat, add the onion, and cook until soft. Add the bacon, potatoes, apples, sage, thyme, salt, and pepper. Gently cook, covered, for 20 minutes, until the apples are soft. Add the liver, parsley, and lemon zest, and cook for 5 minutes. Spread out the stuffing in a wide bowl and let cool.

❧ Meanwhile, make a stock. Put the reserved wing and leg tips and giblets in a saucepan. Add the vegetables, herbs, and peppercorns. Pour in enough cold water to just cover. Slowly bring to a boil, covered, reduce the heat, and simmer with the lid askew for 2 hours.

❧ Preheat the oven to 400°F. Spoon the stuffing into the goose cavity. Insert a small apple at each end to hold the stuffing in place, then seal the flaps with toothpicks. Truss the wings and legs with twine. Put the goose in a roasting pan and cook for 30 minutes, then pour off the fat. Reduce the temperature to 350°F. Cover the goose loosely with aluminum foil and cook for 1¹/₂ hours, pouring off the fat twice again at 30-minute intervals. Add a little water if the pan looks dry. Remove the foil and roast for 30 minutes, until the juices run clear when the thickest part of the thigh is pierced with a sharp knife. Lift the goose onto a warm platter, cover with foil, and let rest for 20 minutes.

❧ To make the gravy, strain 2 cups of stock and blot up any fat that rises. Pour off the fat from the roasting pan. Stir in the cider and vinegar, heat over medium heat, scraping up any sediment in the pan. Add the flour and stir for a minute, until blended. Pour in the strained stock. Bring to a boil, simmer for 5 minutes, and strain.

❧ Slice the apples and arrange around the goose. Carve the goose and serve with the sliced apples, stuffing, and cider gravy.

Chapter 3

VEGETABLES & SIDES

Colcannon

Colcannon is a traditional Irish dish often served at Halloween. In some families, the cook will hide lucky charms or coins in the mixture—these are said to bring the recipients good luck or fortune. This version uses cabbage and scallions, but you can use kale and leeks instead if you prefer.

Serves 4

4 floury potatoes, such as russets or
　Yukon gold, cut into chunks
4 tablespoons lightly salted butter
²/₃ cup light cream
¹/₂ small green or white cabbage
6 scallions, finely chopped
salt and pepper

❧ Cook the potatoes in a large saucepan of boiling salted water for 15–20 minutes. Drain well and mash with a potato masher until smooth. Season to taste with salt and pepper, add the butter and cream, and stir well. The mashed potato should be soft. Keep the potato warm while you cook the cabbage.

❧ Cut the cabbage into quarters, remove the tough core in the middle, and shred the leaves finely. Cook the cabbage in a large saucepan of boiling salted water for 1–2 minutes, until soft. Drain thoroughly.

❧ Mix the potato and cabbage together and stir in the scallions. Season well with salt and pepper.

❧ Serve in individual warm bowls.

Roasted Leeks with Parsley

An all-time Irish favorite, leeks are given a Mediterranean treatment in this quickly prepared dish. Roasted until slightly charred, the leeks make a tasty accompaniment to either fish or roast lamb.

Serves 4

4 large leeks, trimmed and halved
   lengthwise
3 tablespoons extra virgin olive oil
sea salt flakes
black pepper
1 tablespoon chopped fresh
   flat-leaf parsley

❁ Preheat the oven to 475°F. Pack the leeks in a single layer in a shallow casserole dish into which they fit tightly.

❁ Brush with the olive oil, making sure it goes into the crevices. Sprinkle with the sea salt flakes, black pepper, and parsley, turning to coat.

❁ Roast in the preheated oven for 15–20 minutes, turning once, until the leeks begin to blacken at the edges.

Potato Cakes

Potato cakes used to be a way of using up leftover potatoes, but it is worth making some fresh mashed potatoes for this recipe because they will make the cakes particularly light and tasty. They are delicious served hot and smothered with butter.

Serves 4

5 starchy potatoes, such as russets or
  Yukon gold, cut into chunks
2 tablespoons lightly salted butter,
  plus extra to serve
1 egg (optional)
1 cup all-purpose flour
oil, for greasing
salt and pepper

❈ Cook the potatoes in a large saucepan of boiling salted water for 15–20 minutes. Drain well and mash with a potato masher until smooth. Season to taste with salt and pepper and add the butter. Mix in the egg, if using.

❈ Turn the mixture out into a large mixing bowl and add enough of the flour to make a light dough. Work quickly to avoid letting the potatoes cool too much.

❈ Place the dough on a lightly floured surface and roll out carefully to a thickness of $^1/_4$ inch. Using a $2^1/_2$-inch pastry cutter, cut into circles.

❈ Brush a flat griddle pan or heavy skillet with oil and heat. Slip the potato cakes onto the griddle in batches and cook for 4–5 minutes on each side, until they are golden brown.

❈ Serve immediately with butter.

Roasted Beet Packages with Horseradish Butter

Fresh beets are gaining popularity among Irish chefs. In this recipe, the beets are roasted in a foil package, producing wonderfully concentrated flavors and fragrant juices. Horseradish butter makes a piquant contrast to the sweetness of the beets.

Serves 4

8 small beets, peeled and halved
  lengthwise
olive oil
4 thyme sprigs
sea salt flakes
black pepper

Horseradish butter
$^1/_2$ cup (1 stick) unsalted butter,
  at room temperature
$^1/_4$ cup fresh grated horseradish
$^1/_2$ teaspoon sea salt flakes
$^1/_2$ teaspoon black pepper

❖ Preheat the oven to 375°F. Put the beets in a bowl and toss with enough olive oil to coat.

❖ Place four beet halves and a thyme sprig on a thick square of aluminum foil. Season with sea salt flakes and black pepper. Wrap in a loose package, sealing the edges well. Repeat with the remaining beets.

❖ Cook the beets in the preheated oven for about 1 hour, or until you can pierce the beets with a toothpick.

❖ Meanwhile, make the horseradish butter. Mash all the ingredients with a fork, mixing well. Scrape the mixture onto a piece of plastic wrap and form into a log. Chill in the refrigerator.

❖ When the beets are tender, open the foil and add a slice of horseradish butter. Serve immediately, still in the packages.

Glazed Turnips

Ireland's wet climate makes it the perfect place to grow turnips. This much underrated root vegetable is best picked while still small, when the flavor is delicate and slightly sweet. The taste gets stronger as turnips age and the texture becomes coarser, sometimes woody.

Serves 4–6

2 pounds young turnips,
  peeled and quartered
4 tablespoons lightly salted butter
1 tablespoon firmly packed
  light brown sugar
$^2/_3$ cup vegetable stock
1 fresh rosemary sprig
salt and pepper
chopped fresh parsley and grated
  orange rind, to garnish

❈ Put the turnips into a saucepan of boiling salted water, bring back to a boil, and simmer for 10 minutes. Drain well.

❈ Melt the butter in the rinsed-out saucepan over low heat, add the turnips and sugar, and mix to coat well.

❈ Add the stock and the rosemary and bring to a boil. Reduce the heat and simmer for 15–20 minutes, until the liquid has reduced and the turnips are tender and well glazed.

❈ Remove the pan from the heat, remove and discard the rosemary, and season to taste with salt and pepper.

❈ Serve immediately, garnished with the chopped parsley and grated orange rind.

BOTANIC GARDENS, BELFAST

Sticky Carrots with Whiskey & Ginger Glaze

Comforting carrots take on a new lease of life sizzled in butter with snippets of ginger. The juices reduce to a delicious syrupy glaze, while a glug of whiskey gives the dish an Irish touch.

Serves 2–3

1 teaspoon sugar
1/2 teaspoon black pepper
good pinch of sea salt flakes
1/4 cup peanut oil
3 tablespoons lightly salted butter
4 large carrots (about 1 pound),
   diagonally sliced into 1/2-inch circles
3/4-inch piece fresh ginger, sliced into
   matchstick strips
2 tablespoons Irish whiskey
1/2 cup chicken stock or vegetable stock

❧ Combine the sugar, pepper, and sea salt and set aside.

❧ Heat the oil and half of the butter in a large skillet. Add the carrots in a single layer and sprinkle with the sugar mixture. Cook over medium-high heat for 3 minutes, then start turning the slices with tongs and reduce the heat if necessary. When slightly browned on both sides and starting to blacken at the edges, transfer the carrots to a plate.

❧ Clean the skillet with paper towels. Add the ginger and cook over medium-high heat for 1–2 minutes, until golden. Add to the carrots.

❧ Add the remaining butter, the whiskey, and stock. Bring to a boil, then simmer for 3 minutes or until syrupy. Return the carrots and ginger to the skillet, and swirl with the syrup for 1 minute. Serve immediately.

DOLMEN, COUNTY CARLOW (LEFT); GREENFORT, COUNTY DONEGAL (ABOVE)

Sweet & Sour Red Cabbage

Cabbage is a vegetable that is particularly associated with Ireland, although it is only in the last century that so many different varieties have been available. In this tasty recipe, red cabbage is cooked with apples and flavored with spices.

Serves 6–8

1 head red cabbage
2 tablespoons olive oil
2 onions, finely sliced
1 garlic clove, chopped
2 small cooking apples, such as
  Granny Smith or Gravenstein,
  peeled, cored, and sliced
2 tablespoons firmly packed
  dark brown sugar
$\frac{1}{2}$ teaspoon ground cinnamon
1 teaspoon crushed juniper berries
whole nutmeg, for grating
2 tablespoons red wine vinegar
grated rind and juice of 1 orange
2 tablespoons red currant jelly
salt and pepper

- Cut the cabbage into quarters, remove the tough core in the center, and shred the leaves finely.

- Heat the oil in a large saucepan and add the cabbage, onions, garlic, and apples. Stir in the sugar, cinnamon, and juniper berries and grate one-quarter of the nutmeg into the pan.

- Pour over the vinegar and orange juice and add the orange rind. Stir well and season to taste with salt and pepper. The saucepan will be full, but the cabbage will reduce during cooking.

- Cook over medium heat, stirring occasionally, for 10–15 minutes, until the cabbage is just tender but still firm.

- Stir in the red currant jelly, then taste and adjust the seasoning, adding salt and pepper if necessary. Serve immediately.

Bacon & Potato Cakes

Mashed potatoes have been a staple in the Irish kitchen for centuries. In this recipe, they are mixed with bacon snippets and oats, another staple, then fried in cakes until crisp. A topping of watercress sprigs and a strip of crisp bacon gives the cakes a stylish touch.

Serves 4

5 starchy potatoes, such as russets or Yukon gold, peeled and cut into even chunks
8 thin bacon strips
1 tablespoon lightly salted butter
1/2 teaspoon sea salt flakes
1/2 teaspoon black pepper
2 tablespoons snipped chives
1/4 cup rolled oats
1 egg, lightly beaten
all-purpose flour, for dusting
canola oil or vegetable oil, for frying
watercress sprigs, to garnish

- Add the potatoes to a large saucepan of salted boiling water, cover, bring back to a boil, and simmer gently for 20 minutes, until tender. Drain well and put back in the pan. Cover with a clean dish towel for a few minutes to get rid of excess moisture.

- While the potatoes are cooking, cook the bacon over medium-high heat for 5–6 minutes, until crisp. Drain on paper towels. Set aside 4 strips and keep warm. Chop the remaining strips finely.

- Mash the potatoes with the butter, sea salt, and pepper until creamy. Stir in the chopped bacon, chives, oats, and beaten egg.

- With floured hands, form the potato mixture into four flat cakes about 2¾ inches in diameter.

- Heat about ½ inch of oil in a heavy saucepan over medium heat. Add the potato cakes and cook for about 4 minutes on each side, until golden brown.

- Transfer the potato cakes to warm serving plates. Top with the watercress and reserved bacon strips, and serve immediately.

Honeyed Parsnips

In this recipe, oven roasting brings out the natural sweetness of the parsnips, which is then further enhanced by the addition of honey. These parsnips are the perfect accompaniment to any kind of roasted meat.

Serves 4

8 parsnips, peeled and quartered
4 tablespoons vegetable oil
1 tablespoon honey

❀ Preheat the oven to 350°F. Bring a large saucepan of water to the boil. Reduce the heat, add the parsnips, and cook for 5 minutes. Drain thoroughly.

❀ Pour 2 tablespoons of the vegetable oil into a shallow casserole dish and add the parsnips. Mix the remaining oil with the honey and drizzle over the parsnips. Roast in the preheated oven for 45 minutes, until golden brown and tender. Remove from the oven and serve.

THATCHED COTTAGES, COUNTY WATERFORD

Champ

One of Ireland's most delicious side dishes, champ is made with creamy mashed potatoes mixed with chives or scallions, piled high in a bowl with a pool of melted butter in the center. Like Colcannon (page 94), it was traditionally served at Halloween, when it was customary to leave a bowl under a bush for the fairies.

Serves 4

8 starchy potatoes (about 2 pounds), such as russets or Yukon gold, peeled and cut into even chunks
20 scallions, some green tops included, chopped
1½ cups milk
¼ teaspoon white peppercorns
¼ cup snipped chives
1 teaspoon sea salt flakes
½ cup (1 stick) lightly salted butter, melted and hot

❧ Add the potatoes to a large saucepan of salted boiling water, cover, bring back to a boil, and simmer gently for 20 minutes, until tender. Drain well and put back in the pan. Cover with a clean dish towel for a few minutes to get rid of excess moisture.

❧ While the potatoes are cooking, put the chopped scallions in a saucepan with the milk and peppercorns. Simmer for 5 minutes, then drain, reserving the milk and scallions separately.

❧ Mash the potatoes until smooth, stirring in enough of the reserved milk to produce a creamy consistency. Stir in the scallions and chives. Season to taste with sea salt flakes and more pepper if necessary.

❧ Transfer the potato mixture to a warm serving dish. Make a well in the center and pour in the hot, melted butter. Serve immediately, mixing in the melted butter at the table.

Roasted Banana Shallots with Bread Crumbs & Cheddar

A stalwart of Irish cuisine, onions take pride of place in this tasty gratin. Topped with crisp bread crumbs and Irish cheddar cheese, the dish is equally suitable as a vegetarian main course or an accompaniment to roast beef or lamb.

Serves 4–6

8 banana shallots or small-to-medium onions
2 tablespoons apple juice concentrate
6 tablespoons olive oil or canola oil
1/2 tablespoon finely chopped fresh thyme or rosemary
1/4 teaspoon black pepper
sea salt flakes
2/3 cup coarse stale bread crumbs
1 cup shredded mild Irish cheddar cheese
1 tablespoon chopped fresh parsley, to garnish

❦ Preheat the oven to 425°F. Peel the banana shallots, slice in half lengthwise, and put in a shallow bowl.

❦ Whisk together the apple juice concentrate, 4 tablespoons of the olive oil, and the thyme. Pour the mixture over the shallots, turning to coat well.

❦ Transfer the contents of the bowl into a small nonstick roasting pan in which the shallots fit in a single layer. Turn the shallots cut-side up and season with the pepper and a good pinch of sea salt flakes. Sprinkle with the bread crumbs and the remaining oil.

❦ Roast in the preheated oven for 25–30 minutes, or until the shallots are soft and the edges are beginning to blacken. Scatter the shredded cheese over the top, and roast for an additional 3 minutes, or until the cheese is melted and bubbling.

❦ Garnish with the parsley and serve immediately.

Buttered Kale with Chives & Lemon

Kale is a sturdy crop that features regularly on the Irish menu, particularly in winter. In this recipe, it is lightly cooked and seasoned with lemon zest and chives to complement the rich and earthy flavor.

Serves 4–6

8 ounces kale
grated zest of 1 lemon
¹/₃ cup snipped chives
large pat of lightly salted butter
sea salt flakes
white pepper

- Remove the tough stems from the kale, then stack the leaves and slice into wide ribbons. Place in a steamer basket set over boiling water. Steam for 10–12 minutes, until tender but still bright green.

- Transfer the kale to a warm serving dish, add the lemon zest, chives, and butter, and toss together. Season with sea salt flakes and pepper. Serve immediately.

TRADITIONAL HOUSE, COUNTY WICKLOW

Red Cabbage with Mushrooms, Nuts & Bacon

A major feature of Irish cuisine, cabbage comes in a cornucopia of appetizing colors and flavors. In this recipe, red cabbage is lightly braised with bacon, mushrooms, and crunchy nuts and is a superb accompaniment to roast goose or pork.

Serves 4

1/2 large red cabbage
2 tablespoons canola oil or vegetable oil
6 thin bacon strips, cut into
   bite-size pieces
1 onion, chopped
2 teaspoons thyme leaves
2 1/2 cups coarsely chopped cremini
   mushrooms
1/3 cup toasted hazelnuts, coarsely
   chopped
grated zest of 1 lemon
1 teaspoon sea salt flakes
1/2 teaspoon black pepper
1/2 teaspoon sugar
2 tablespoons apple cider vinegar
1 cup meat stock
1/4 cup chopped fresh parsley
pat of lightly salted butter

❧ Quarter the cabbage lengthwise and discard the tough core in the center. Slice the leaves widthwise into ribbons.

❧ Heat the oil in a flameproof casserole dish or deep skillet over medium-high heat. Cook the bacon for about 5 minutes, until crisp.

❧ Reduce the heat to medium, add the onion and thyme, and cook for 5 minutes, until the onion is translucent.

❧ Add the mushrooms and cabbage, and cook for an additional 5 minutes, until starting to soften.

❧ Stir in the nuts, lemon zest, sea salt, pepper, and sugar, and cook for an additional 3 minutes. Pour in the vinegar and stock, cover, and bring to a boil, then reduce the heat and simmer for 15 minutes, until the cabbage is tender.

❧ Check the seasoning, adding salt and pepper if necessary. Stir in the parsley and a pat of butter just before serving.

CAUSEWAY COASTAL ROUTE, COUNTY ANTRIM (LEFT); RIVER IN IRELAND (ABOVE)

Irish Soda Bread

Soda bread has long been a staple in Ireland. It is a bread made without yeast, because baking soda mixed with buttermilk is used as a leavening agent. A cross is cut into the top of the bread to help it rise and, according to Irish folklore, to either ward off evil or let the fairies out.

Makes 1 loaf

vegetable oil, for oiling
3²/₃ cups all-purpose flour,
  plus extra for dusting
1 teaspoon salt
1 teaspoon baking soda
1³/₄ cups buttermilk

❊ Preheat the oven to 425°F. Oil a baking sheet.

❊ Sift the flour, salt, and baking soda into a mixing bowl. Make a well in the center and pour in most of the buttermilk. Mix together well using your hands. The dough should be soft but not too wet. If necessary, add the remaining buttermilk.

❊ Turn the dough out onto a lightly floured surface and knead it lightly. Shape into a 8-inch circle. Place the loaf on the prepared baking sheet and cut a cross into the top with a sharp knife.

❊ Bake in the preheated oven for 25–30 minutes, until golden brown and it sounds hollow when tapped on the bottom. Transfer to a wire rack and let cool slightly. Serve warm.

TRIM CASTLE, COUNTY MEATH

Brown Soda Bread
with Molasses

In rural Ireland bread was always made at home. It was baked on the griddle or in a cooking pot, and was usually dense-textured as yeast was rarely used as the raising agent. The introduction of baking soda in the nineteenth century made it possible for families to produce quickly made risen bread for which Ireland is now famous.

Makes 1 loaf

2 cups all-purpose flour,
 plus extra for dusting
2 cups whole wheat flour
$1/2$ cup rolled oats
$1^1/2$ teaspoons salt
1 teaspoon baking soda
$1^3/4$ cups buttermilk
2 tablespoons molasses

✖ Preheat the oven to 450°F. Line a baking sheet with a sheet of nonstick parchment paper.

✖ Combine the flours, oats, salt, and baking soda in a large bowl, mixing thoroughly.

✖ Whisk together the buttermilk and molasses in a large pitcher. Make a well in the center of the flour mixture and pour in the buttermilk mixture. Using a fork, stir the liquid, gradually drawing in the flour from around the edge. With floured hands, lightly knead to a soft dough.

✖ Shape the dough into a circle and place on the lined baking sheet. Press flat to about 2 inches thick. Use a sharp knife with a long blade to cut a deep cross on the top.

✖ Bake in the preheated oven for 15 minutes, then reduce the oven temperature to 400°F. Bake for an additional 20-25 minutes, or until the bottom of the bread sounds hollow when tapped. Transfer to a wire rack and let cool slightly. Serve warm.

Oat & Potato Bread

This recipe uses freshly cooked potatoes, but it is also a wonderful way to use up leftover mashed potatoes. It makes a dense, moist loaf that is the perfect accompaniment to any meal, although it is particularly delicious served with a traditional Irish hot breakfast.

Makes 1 loaf

vegetable oil, for oiling

2 starchy potatoes, such as russets or
   Yukon gold, cut into even chunks

$3^2/_3$ cups white bread flour,
   plus extra for dusting

$1^1/_2$ teaspoons salt

3 tablespoons lightly salted butter, diced

$1^1/_2$ teaspoons active dry yeast

$1^1/_2$ tablespoons firmly packed
   dark brown sugar

3 tablespoons rolled oats

2 tablespoons dry skim milk

1 cup lukewarm water

Topping

1 tablepoon water

1 tablespoon rolled oats

❖ Oil a 9-inch loaf pan. Put the potatoes in a large saucepan, add water to cover, and bring to a boil. Cook for 20–25 minutes, until tender. Drain, then mash until smooth. Let cool.

❖ Sift the flour and salt into a warm bowl. Rub in the butter with your fingertips. Stir in the yeast, sugar, oats, and dry milk. Mix in the mashed potatoes, then add the water and mix to a soft dough.

❖ Turn out the dough onto a lightly floured surface and knead for 5–10 minutes, or until smooth and elastic. Put the dough in an oiled bowl, cover with plastic wrap, and let rise in a warm place for 1 hour, or until doubled in size.

❖ Invert the dough onto a lightly floured surface and knead lightly. Shape into a loaf and transfer to the prepared pan. Cover and let rise in a warm place for 30 minutes. Meanwhile, preheat the oven to 425°F.

❖ Brush the surface of the loaf with the water and carefully sprinkle over the oats. Bake in the preheated oven for 25–30 minutes, or until it sounds hollow when tapped on the bottom. Transfer to a wire rack and let cool slightly. Serve warm.

Barm Brack

Barm Brack is a yeast bread with added raisins—it is sweeter than standard bread but not as rich as cake. It is traditionally eaten around Halloween, when charms are baked into the dough as part of an ancient fortune-telling ritual.

Makes 1 loaf

4³/₄ cups white bread flour,
  plus extra for dusting
1 teaspoon allspice
1 teaspoon salt
2 teaspoons active dry yeast
1 tablespoon sugar
1¹/₄ cups lukewarm milk
²/₃ cup lukewarm water
vegetable oil, for oiling
4 tablespoons lightly salted butter,
  softened, plus extra to serve
1³/₄ cups mixed dried fruit, such
  as golden raisins, dried currants,
  and raisins
milk, for glazing

❀ Sift the flour, allspice, and salt into a warm bowl. Stir in the yeast and sugar. Make a well in the center and pour in the milk and water. Mix well to make a sticky dough. Turn the dough out onto a lightly floured work surface and knead until no longer sticky. Put the dough in an oiled bowl, cover with plastic wrap, and let rise in a warm place for 1 hour, until doubled in size.

❀ Turn the dough out onto a floured work surface and knead lightly for 1 minute. Add the butter and dried fruit to the dough and work them in until completely incorporated. Return the dough to the bowl, replace the plastic wrap, and let rise for 30 minutes.

❀ Oil a 9-inch round cake pan. Pat the dough to a neat circle and fit in the pan. Cover and let rest in a warm place until it has risen to the top of the pan. Meanwhile, preheat the oven to 400°F.

❀ Brush the top of the loaf lightly with milk and bake in the preheated oven for 15 minutes. Cover the loaf with aluminum foil, reduce the oven temperature to 350°F, and bake for an additional 45 minutes, until golden brown and it sounds hollow when tapped on the bottom. Transfer to a wire rack and let cool.

❀ Serve sliced and spread with butter.

Boxty Bread

The Irish have always been adept at baking, making do with the simplest of ingredients and equipment. This traditional bread is made with potato and wheat flour dough, shaped into flat circles. It makes a delicious afternoon snack served warm with plenty of butter or cheese and pickles.

Makes 4 small loaves

7 starchy potatoes (about 1³/₄ pounds), such as russets or Yukon gold

2 tablespoons lightly salted butter, plus extra to serve

²/₃ cup milk

2 teaspoons salt

¹/₂ teaspoon black pepper

1¹/₂ teaspoons dill seeds or caraway seeds (optional)

2³/₄ cups all-purpose flour, plus extra for dusting

5 teaspoons baking powder

❇ Preheat the oven to 375°F. Peel four of the potatoes, cut them into even chunks, and bring to a boil in a large saucepan of salted water. Cover and simmer gently for about 20 minutes, until tender. Drain well and put back in the pan. Cover with a clean dish towel for a few minutes to get rid of excess moisture. Mash with the butter until smooth.

❇ Meanwhile, peel the remaining three potatoes and grate coarsely. Wrap in a clean piece of cheesecloth and squeeze tightly to remove the moisture. Put the grated potatoes in a large bowl with the milk, ³/₄ teaspoon of the salt, the pepper, and dill seeds, if using. Beat in the mashed potatoes.

❇ Sift the flour, baking powder, and remaining salt onto the potato mixture. Mix to a smooth dough, adding a little more flour if the mixture is too soft.

❇ Knead lightly, then shape into four flat, round loaves about 4 inches in diameter. Place on a nonstick baking sheet. Mark each loaf with a large cross. Bake in the preheated oven for 40 minutes, or until well-risen and golden brown.

❇ Break each loaf into quarters. Serve warm, spread with butter.

Oat Crackers

These crunchy oat crackers, with added walnuts and sesame seeds, are quick and easy to make. They would be the ideal accompaniment for a cheese board—make sure to include a range of Irish cheeses and some chutney or other relishes.

Makes 12–14

7 tablespoons unsalted butter,
  plus extra for greasing
1 cup rolled oats
3 tablespoons whole wheat flour
1/2 teaspoon coarse sea salt
1 teaspoon dried thyme
1/3 cup finely chopped walnuts
1 egg, beaten
1/4 cup sesame seeds

❖ Preheat the oven to 350°F. Lightly grease two baking sheets.

❖ Rub the butter into the oats and flour using your fingertips. Stir in the salt, thyme, and walnuts, then add the egg and mix to a soft dough. Spread out the sesame seeds on a large shallow plate. Break off walnut-size pieces of dough and roll into balls, then roll in the sesame seeds to coat lightly and evenly.

❖ Place the balls of dough on the prepared baking sheets, spacing well apart, and roll a rolling pin over them to flatten. Bake in the preheated oven for 12–15 minutes, or until firm and pale golden. Transfer to a wire rack and let cool.

GIANT'S CAUSEWAY, COUNTY ANTRIM

Chapter 4

DESSERTS & DRINKS

Irish Whiskey Trifle

Trifle is said to have a "powerful stronghold" in Ireland, with every family having its favorite recipe that is, of course, better than anyone else's. This version contains the usual Irish whiskey and sherry, but you could use fruit juice for soaking if you prefer a nonalcoholic version.

Serves 8

10 ladyfingers or 1 stale sponge cake
raspberry jam, for spreading
2 macaroons, lightly crushed
finely grated zest of 1 lemon
2 tablespoons Irish whiskey
$^1/_2$ cup sherry
$1^1/_4$ cups heavy cream
$^1/_2$ tablespoon sugar
1 cup raspberries
candied violets or miniature macaroons,
   to decorate

Custard
5 egg yolks, lightly beaten
$^1/_4$ cup sugar
2 teaspoons cornstarch
$^1/_2$ cup whole milk
1 cup heavy cream
$^1/_2$ teaspoon vanilla extract

- First make the custard. Combine the egg yolks and sugar in a mixing bowl. Stir in the cornstarch and mix to a smooth paste, then whisk in the milk.

- Heat the cream in a heavy saucepan until just starting to simmer but not boiling. Gradually whisk the hot cream into the egg mixture, then return the mixture to the pan. Whisk continuously over medium heat for about 5 minutes, until thickened. Immediately pour into a pitcher and stir in the vanilla extract. Cover with plastic wrap to prevent a skin from forming and let stand to cool completely.

- Thickly spread half of the ladyfingers with raspberry jam. Place the remaining ladyfingers on top to make a sandwich. If using sponge cake, slice horizontally into two or three layers and spread with jam. Arrange in a single layer in the bottom of a deep serving dish. Sprinkle with the crushed macaroons and the lemon zest.

- Combine the whiskey and sherry and pour over the ladyfinger mixture. Let soak for 1 hour.

- Spoon the cooled custard over the ladyfinger mixture.

- Whip the cream with the sugar until stiff peaks form. Spread over the custard, leveling with a spatula. Cover with plastic wrap and chill for 1 hour, or until ready to serve.

- Arrange the raspberries on top and decorate with candied violets or miniature macaroons.

Bread & Butter Pudding

Warm and comforting, bread and butter pudding is the perfect dessert for a cold winter's day. It was traditionally made with dry leftover bread, but this luxury version uses fresh bread—you could also try using fruit bread.

Serves 4–6

6 tablespoons lightly salted butter, softened
6 slices thick white bread
$1/3$ cup mixed dried fruit, such as golden raisins, currants, and raisins
2 tablespoons candied peel
3 extra-large eggs
$1^1/4$ cups milk
$2/3$ cup heavy cream
$1/4$ cup granulated sugar
whole nutmeg, for grating
1 tablespoon demerara sugar or other raw sugar

❅ Preheat the oven to 350°F. Use a little of the butter to grease an 8 x 10-inch baking dish and the remainder to butter the slices of bread. Cut the bread diagonally into quarters and arrange half of them overlapping in the prepared baking dish.

❅ Scatter half of the dried fruit and candied peel over the bread, cover with the remaining bread slices, and add the remaining dried fruit and candied peel.

❅ Whisk the eggs well in a large pitcher, then mix in the milk, cream, and granulated sugar. Pour the mixture over the bread and let stand for 15 minutes so the bread soaks up some of the egg mixture.

❅ Tuck the dried fruit and candied peel under the bread slices so they don't burn. Grate a little of the nutmeg over the top of the bread, according to taste, and sprinkle over the demerara sugar.

❅ Place the dish on a baking sheet and bake at the top of the preheated oven for 30–40 minutes, until just set and golden brown. Remove from the oven and serve warm.

Apple Cake

Apples have been grown in Ireland for many centuries—legend has it that St. Patrick himself planted an apple tree in an ancient settlement outside Armagh city. Today, County Armagh is known as "Orchard County" and celebrates its apples with festivals and apple-blossom tours. This cake is a tasty way of using apples and can be served warm for dessert.

Serves 8

2 large cooking apples, such as Granny Smith or Gravenstein
1 1/3 cups all-purpose flour
2 teaspoons baking powder
1 teaspoon ground cinnamon
1/2 teaspoon salt
1/2 cup (1 stick) lightly salted butter, plus extra for greasing
1/2 cup plus 1 tablespoon superfine sugar (or the same amount of granulated sugar processed in a blender or food processor for 1 minute)
2 eggs
1–2 tablespoons milk
confectioners' sugar, for dusting

Streusel topping

1 cup all-purpose flour
6 tablespoons butter
1/2 cup superfine sugar

- Preheat the oven to 350°F and grease a 9-inch round springform cake pan.
- To make the streusel topping, sift the flour into a bowl and rub in the butter until the mixture resembles bread crumbs. Stir in the sugar and reserve.
- Peel, core, and thinly slice the apples. To make the cake, sift the flour into a bowl with the baking powder, cinnamon, and salt. Place the butter and superfine sugar in a separate bowl and beat together until light and fluffy. Gradually beat in the eggs, adding a little of the flour mixture with the last addition of egg. Gently fold in half of the remaining flour mixture, then fold in the rest with the milk.
- Spoon the batter into the prepared pan and smooth the top. Cover with the sliced apples and sprinkle the streusel topping evenly over the top. Bake in the preheated oven for 1 hour, or until browned and firm to the touch. Let cool in the pan before removing the sides. Dust the cake with confectioners' sugar before serving.

Oatmeal & Raspberry Cream

Oats became important to the Irish during the potato famine in the mid-nineteenth century. In this recipe, they are folded into an irresistible concoction of raspberries and whiskey- and honey-flavored cream. The dish was traditionally served to celebrate the end of the annual harvest. It is rich, so the portions are small.

Serves 6

1 cup rolled oats
1 1/2 cups heavy cream
1/2 cup light cream
3 tablespoons Irish whiskey
2 tablespoons honey,
   plus extra for drizzling
2 1/2 cups raspberries

❧ Preheat the broiler to medium. Spread out the oats on a baking sheet, place under the preheated broiler, and toast for 4–5 minutes, or until golden brown, stirring often to prevent burning. Transfer to a shallow bowl and let cool.

❧ Combine the two creams, whiskey, and honey in a mixing bowl. Stir in the oats, mixing well. Cover with plastic wrap and let rest in the refrigerator for at least 2 hours or overnight to thicken. Stir occasionally to break up any clumps of oats.

❧ Set aside 1/3 cup of the best raspberries to decorate. Lightly swirl the remaining raspberries into the oat mixture, creating attractive pink streaks. Spoon into glass serving dishes and decorate with the reserved raspberries. Drizzle with honey just before serving.

Rhubarb Crisp

This comforting dessert is incredibly simple to make—you can even make the crisp topping a day or two in advance and store it in the refrigerator until you are ready to use it. For an extra-crunchy topping, use demerara sugar or other raw sugar in place of the light brown sugar.

Serves 6

2 pounds rhubarb
$^1/_2$ cup granulated sugar
grated rind and juice of 1 orange
cream, yogurt, or custard, to serve

Crisp topping
1$^3/_4$ cups all-purpose white or
   whole wheat flour
$^1/_2$ cup unsalted butter
$^1/_2$ cup firmly packed light brown sugar
1 teaspoon ground ginger

❧ Preheat the oven to 375°F. Cut the rhubarb into 1-inch lengths and place in a 2-quart casserole dish with the sugar and orange rind and juice.

❧ To make the crisp topping, sift the flour into a bowl. Rub in the butter with your fingertips until the mixture resembles fine bread crumbs. Stir in the brown sugar and ginger. Spread evenly over the fruit and press down lightly using a fork.

❧ Place the dish on a baking sheet and bake in the preheated oven for 25–30 minutes, until the topping is golden brown. Serve warm with cream, yogurt, or stirred custard.

UPPER LAKE, KILLARNEY NATIONAL PARK, COUNTY KERRY

Blackberry Soup with Buttermilk Custards

Dried carrageen (Irish moss) would traditionally have been used as a thickening agent for custards and milk puddings, but this recipe uses the more readily available gelatin. The sweet and inky blackberry soup and wobbly buttermilk custard are a sublime combination.

Serves 4

Buttermilk custards
4 sheets or about 1¼ envelopes
  unflavored gelatin
1 cup plus 3 tablespoons buttermilk
1 cup plus 3 tablespoons heavy cream
¼ cup whole milk
½ cup sugar

Blackberry soup
3 cups blackberries
1¼ cups fruity red wine
½ cup water
⅓ cup sugar, or to taste
2 star anise
¼–⅓ cup blackberry liqueur (optional)

❖ To make the custards, put the gelatin in a small bowl, cover with cold water, and let soak for 5 minutes. Meanwhile, heat the buttermilk, cream, and milk together in a saucepan to just below boiling point. Add the sugar and stir until it has completely dissolved. Remove the gelatin from the soaking liquid and squeeze out any excess water. Add to the hot buttermilk mixture and stir until completely dissolved. Pour through a fine strainer and fill four dariole molds or individual dessert molds. Transfer to the refrigerator and chill for several hours, or overnight, until set.

❖ To make the blackberry soup, put the blackberries, wine, and water in a large saucepan with the sugar and star anise. Simmer gently for 8–10 minutes, until the sugar has dissolved and the mixture has a lovely anise scent. Remove from the heat and let cool. Once the mixture has cooled, remove and discard the star anise, transfer the mixture to a food processor, and blend until smooth. Pour through a fine strainer and stir in the liqueur, if using. Cover and chill in the refrigerator until ready to serve.

❖ To serve, divide the blackberry soup among four shallow bowls and place a buttermilk custard in the center of each.

Irish Cream Cheesecake

This is an unbaked cheesecake and, although it contains no gelatin, its high chocolate content guarantees that it sets perfectly. It is a luxurious dessert that is made even more special by the addition of Irish Cream, a popular liqueur made from Irish whiskey, coffee, and cream.

Serves 8

vegetable oil, for oiling
4 tablespoons unsalted butter
1½ cups crushed chocolate chip cookies
crème fraîche or whipped cream and
  fresh strawberries, to serve

Filling

8 ounces semisweet dark chocolate,
  broken into pieces
8 ounces milk chocolate, broken
  into pieces
¼ cup sugar
1½ cups cream cheese
2 cups heavy cream, lightly whipped
3 tablespoons Irish Cream liqueur

❧ Line the bottom of an 8-inch round springform cake pan with parchment paper and brush the sides with oil. Put the butter in a saucepan and heat gently until melted. Stir in the crushed cookies. Press into the bottom of the prepared cake pan and chill in the refrigerator for 1 hour.

❧ To make the filling, put the dark and milk chocolates into a heatproof bowl set over a saucepan of gently simmering water until melted. Let cool. Put the sugar and cream cheese in a bowl and beat together until smooth, then fold in the cream. Fold the melted chocolate into the cream cheese mixture, then stir in the liqueur.

❧ Spoon into the cake pan and smooth the surface. Let chill in the refrigerator for 2 hours, or until firm. Transfer to a serving plate and cut into slices. Serve with crème fraîche and strawberries.

Chocolate & Stout Ice Cream

This extremely rich, dark ice cream is perfect for a St. Patrick's Day celebration. Served cold, the stout flavor is subtle and perfectly matched by dark, bittersweet chocolate. For an extra-special touch, splash a little Irish Cream liqueur over each serving.

Makes about 3½ cups

1½ cups whole milk
¾ cup sugar
5½ ounces semisweet dark chocolate (at least 85 percent cocoa solids), broken into small pieces
4 egg yolks
1 teaspoon vanilla extract
1⅓ cups stout
1 cup heavy cream
grated chocolate, to decorate

❧ Pour the milk into a saucepan and add the sugar. Bring to a boil, stirring, until the sugar has dissolved. Remove from the heat and stir in the chocolate.

❧ Pour the egg yolks into a heatproof bowl and beat for 5 minutes, or until the beaters leave a faint trail when lifted from the mixture. Stir some of the warm chocolate mixture into the egg yolks, then gradually beat in the rest.

❧ Place the bowl over a saucepan of gently boiling water. Stir continuously for about 10 minutes, until the mixture reaches a temperature of 185°F, or is thick enough to coat the back of a spoon. Be careful not to let it boil.

❧ Strain the mixture through a fine strainer into a pitcher. Stir in the vanilla extract. Sit the bottom of the pitcher in iced water until cold, then cover with plastic wrap and chill for 2 hours.

❧ Meanwhile, pour the stout into a saucepan and bring to a boil. Reduce the heat and simmer briskly for 8 minutes, until reduced to 1 cup. Pour into a pitcher, let cool, then chill in the refrigerator.

❧ Stir the cream and chilled stout into the chocolate mixture, mixing well. Pour the mixture into the bowl of an ice cream machine. Churn and freeze following the manufacturer's instructions. Alternatively, pour the mixture into a shallow freezerproof container, cover with plastic wrap, and freeze for about 2 hours, until beginning to harden around the edges. Beat until smooth to get rid of any ice crystals. Freeze again, repeat the process twice, then freeze until completely firm.

❧ Move the ice cream to the refrigerator 30 minutes before serving to soften. Serve in chilled dishes, sprinkled with grated chocolate.

TRADITIONAL PUBS IN DUBLIN AND GALWAY

Irish Spiced Fruitcake

This traditional cake is a typical Irish afternoon treat.
Unsweetened dried cherries give it a pleasing tang, as do ginger
and allspice. The cake will keep for several days wrapped in
wax paper and stored in an airtight container.

Makes one 8-inch cake

1½ cups mixed dried fruit, such as
   golden raisins, currants, and raisins
⅔ cup dried unsweetened cherries
⅓ cup coarsely chopped walnuts
¾ cup demerara sugar or other
   raw sugar
½ cup (1 stick) butter
1 teaspoon allspice
1 teaspoon ground ginger
½ teaspoon baking soda
1 cup milk
1¾ cups self-rising flour
2 eggs, lightly beaten

❈ Put all the ingredients apart from the flour and eggs into a saucepan and mix well. Bring to a boil over medium-high heat, stirring continuously. Reduce the heat slightly and simmer for 5 minutes, stirring occasionally. Remove from the heat and let cool for about 30 minutes.

❈ Meanwhile, preheat the oven to 350°F. Grease and line a deep 8-inch cake pan.

❈ Add the flour and eggs to the cake batter, mixing well to combine. Spoon the batter into the prepared pan, leveling the surface with a wet spatula.

❈ Bake in the preheated oven for 30 minutes. Reduce the oven temperature to 325°F and bake for an additional 1½ hours, or until a toothpick inserted in the center comes out clean.

❈ Let the cake cool in the pan for 10 minutes, then invert onto a wire rack and let cool completely.

Porter Cake

Porter, or stout, is a special type of dark beer first brewed in Ireland in the eighteenth century. Guinness is an extra-strong porter that provides color and flavor without being too overwhelming. Stored in an airtight container, this rich, moist fruitcake is best eaten several days after baking.

Makes one 7-inch cake

3 cups mixed currants and golden raisins
1 cup dried unsweetened cherries
¾ cup finely chopped candied citrus peel
1⅓ cups stout
2¾ cups all-purpose flour
1 teaspoon baking powder
1 teaspoon allspice
pinch of salt
1 cup (2 sticks) butter
1 cup firmly packed brown sugar
3 eggs, lightly beaten

❧ Mix the currants, golden raisins, cherries, and citrus peel in a large bowl. Add the stout and let soak for at least 5 hours or overnight, stirring occasionally.

❧ Preheat the oven to 325°F. Grease and line a 7-inch square cake pan.

❧ Sift the flour, baking powder, spice, and salt into a large bowl.

❧ Cream the butter and sugar in a separate bowl for about 4 minutes, until light and fluffy. Stir in the beaten eggs, a little at a time, adding some of the flour mixture at each addition and beating well. Stir in the remaining flour.

❧ Add the fruit and any liquid to the batter, mixing well to a soft consistency. Spoon the batter into the prepared pan, leveling the surface with a wet spatula.

❧ Bake in the preheated oven for 1 hour. Reduce the oven temperature to 300°F and bake for an additional 1½–2 hours, or until a toothpick inserted in the center comes out clean. Let rest in the pan until completely cool.

❧ Invert, wrap in wax paper, and store in an airtight container.

Molasses Bread

Popular throughout Ireland, where it's called treacle bread—in this recipe, the treacle is replaced with molasses—this moist, dense quick bread is easy to make and keeps well. It is always served thickly spread with butter, and invariably comes with a strong cup of tea. It is also delicious spread with cream cheese.

Makes 1 loaf

1³/₄ cups all-purpose flour

1 teaspoon baking soda

¹/₂ teaspoon allspice

¹/₂ teaspoon ground ginger

5 tablespoons lightly salted butter, plus extra to serve

3 tablespoons molasses

2 eggs, lightly beaten

¹/₄ cup buttermilk

¹/₂ cup firmly packed brown sugar

¹/₃ cup currants

¹/₃ cup golden raisins

- Preheat the oven to 350°F. Grease and line a small 6¹/₂-x 3³/₄-inch loaf pan.

- Sift the flour, baking soda, and spices into a bowl. Lightly rub in the butter until the mixture resembles fine crumbs.

- Whisk the molasses with the eggs and buttermilk, then stir in the sugar. Make a well in the center of the flour mixture and pour in the molasses mixture. Mix with a fork, gradually drawing in the flour from around the edges.

- Add the currants and golden raisins, and mix to a soft dough. Spoon the dough into the prepared loaf pan, leveling the surface with a wet spatula.

- Bake in the preheated oven for 45–55 minutes, or until a toothpick inserted in the center comes out clean.

- Let cool in the pan for 15 minutes, then invert onto a wire rack and let rest for about 2 hours to cool completely.

- Serve spread thickly with butter.

Currant Shortbread

Shortbread is usually associated with Scotland, but similar versions are made throughout Ireland. As with many Irish dishes, each region, and often each family, has its own treasured recipe. This one includes currants and lemon zest for flavor, and ground rice for crunch.

Makes 12 wedges

1⅓ cups all-purpose flour
pinch of salt
½ cup ground rice or fine semolina
¾ cup (1½ sticks) lightly salted butter, softened
⅓ cup superfine sugar, plus extra for dredging
finely grated zest of 1 lemon
¼ cup dried currants

❇ Preheat the oven to 325°F. Sift the flour and salt into a bowl, and mix in the ground rice.

❇ Beat together the butter, sugar, and lemon zest in a separate bowl. Stir in the flour mixture and currants. Work the dough with your hands until it clumps together. Mold into a flattened ball and place on a nonstick baking sheet.

❇ Use your fingers to press the dough into a 9½-inch circle (use a small dinner plate as a guide). Lightly level the surface with a rolling pin and trim the edges neatly. Make indentations around the edge with the back of a fork, and prick the surface all over to stop it from puffing up. Mark the top into 12 equal segments with a knife.

❇ Bake in the preheated oven for 30–35 minutes, or until pale golden all over.

❇ Remove from the oven and dredge with sugar. Cut through the marked segments, then let cool and firm up.

Custard Tarts

Custard tarts are a familiar sight in Irish bakeries. This version, made with crisp, light puff pastry and a cinnamon-scented filling, is similar to the Portuguese custard tarts that are increasingly popular among modern chefs. The tarts are best eaten on the day they're made, preferably while still warm.

Serves 12

butter, for greasing
5 egg yolks, lightly beaten
$\frac{1}{2}$ cup superfine sugar (or the same quantity granulated sugar processed in a blender or food processor for 1 minute)
2 teaspoons cornstarch
$\frac{1}{2}$ cup whole milk
1 cup heavy cream
2-inch cinnamon stick
2 strips orange peel
$\frac{1}{2}$ teaspoon vanilla extract
13 ounces store-bought puff pastry
freshly grated nutmeg, for sprinkling
flour, for dusting

❧ Preheat the oven to 375°F. Lightly grease a 12-cup muffin pan. Combine the egg yolks and sugar in a mixing bowl. Stir in the cornstarch and mix to a smooth paste, then whisk in the milk.

❧ Heat the cream in a heavy saucepan until just starting to simmer but not boiling. Gradually whisk the hot cream into the egg mixture, then return the mixture to the pan. Add the cinnamon stick and orange peel. Whisk continuously over medium heat for about 5 minutes, until thickened. Immediately pour into a pitcher. Stir in the vanilla extract. Cover with plastic wrap to prevent a skin from forming and set aside.

❧ Place the sheet of puff pastry on a board and trim to a rectangle measuring about 11 x 9$\frac{1}{2}$ inches. Discard the trimmings or use in another recipe. Slice in half lengthwise to make two rectangles, each measuring 11 x 4$\frac{3}{4}$ inches. Sprinkle one rectangle with freshly grated nutmeg. Place the other on top to make a sandwich. Roll up from the narrow end to make a log. Using a sharp knife, cut the log into twelve half-inch slices.

❧ Roll out the slices on a floured board to 4$\frac{1}{2}$-inch circles. Place the circles in the muffin-pan cups, lightly pressing down into the bottom and leaving a slightly thicker rim around the top edge.

❧ Remove the cinnamon stick and orange peel from the custard and discard. Pour the custard into the pastry shells.

❧ Bake for 20 minutes, or until the crust and filling are golden brown. Let the tarts cool in the pan for 5 minutes, then transfer to a wire rack to cool.

Irish Coffee

Irish coffee is a cocktail made with strong, hot coffee, Irish whiskey, and sugar, topped with thick cream. It is the perfect way to round off a meal or to ward off the night's chill. You'll need a steady hand to get the cream to float on top, but practice makes perfect!

Serves 1

2 measures Irish whiskey
1 teaspoon sugar, or more to taste
freshly made strong black coffee
2 measures heavy cream

- Put the whiskey into a warm heatproof glass with sugar to taste.
- Pour in the coffee and stir until the sugar has completely dissolved. Pour the cream slowly over the back of a spoon that is just touching the top of the coffee and the edge of the glass. Keep pouring until all the cream is added and has settled on the top.
- Do not stir—drink the coffee through the cream.

TORC WATERFALL,

Black Velvet

This beer cocktail is made using equal measures of stout and sparkling white wine (traditionally Guinness and champagne). The different densities of the liquids mean that they should, in theory at least, remain in separate layers, as in a *pousse-café*. For a Poor Man's Black Velvet, use hard cider instead of the wine, pouring it into the glass first and floating the stout on top.

Serves 1

stout, chilled
sparkling white wine, chilled

Fill a glass half-full of stout, then slowly pour in an equal quantity of wine over the back of a spoon that is just touching the top of the stout and the edge of the glass. This should prevent the drinks from mixing together too much and help to keep them in separate layers. Serve immediately.

BUNRATTY FOLK PARK, COUNTY CLARE

Scailtin (Milk Punch)

Ireland is famous for its dairy products and its whiskey. In this recipe, the two are combined in a hot, spicy punch that will warm the cockles of your heart.

Serves 2

2 cups whole milk
¹/₂ cup Irish whiskey
1–2 tablespoons honey, or to taste
¹/₈ teaspoon ground ginger
¹/₈ teaspoon ground cinnamon
freshly grated nutmeg, to decorate

❈ Pour the milk and whiskey into a small saucepan and stir in the honey, ginger, and cinnamon.

❈ Heat slowly, without letting the mixture boil, whisking briskly all the time to create a froth and to disperse the ground spices.

❈ Pour into two warm mugs and sprinkle with grated nutmeg.

Whiskey & Orange Oat Cream Toddy

Hot, whiskey-spiked orange juice is topped with Ireland's favorite ingredients: thick cream and crunchy toasted oats. Serve it as a special nightcap on a chilly winter evening.

Serves 2

freshly squeezed juice of 6
   large oranges
1–1¹/₂ tablespoons honey, or to taste
¹/₂ cup heavy cream
3 tablespoons Irish whiskey
1¹/₂ tablespoons rolled oats, toasted

❊ Squeeze the juice from the oranges. There should be about 1¹/₂ cups.

❊ Strain the juice into a small saucepan. Add the honey and heat until hot but not boiling.

❊ Whip the cream lightly until soft peaks form. Stir in 1 tablespoon of the whiskey.

❊ Add the remaining 2 tablespoons of whiskey to the hot orange juice.

❊ Pour the mixture into 2 warm whiskey glasses. Top with a layer of whipped cream and sprinkle with toasted oats.

FOUR COURTS, DUBLIN

Index